W9-CZU-929

Vine Street Public Landing
Brittons
Smiths
Brooks
Sassafras Street Public Landing
Hams
Warner
Platt
Hodge
Smith Paul
Halterbach Slinemetz
Fisher Peddle Robbins
Mulberry Street Ferry and Public L
Old Ferry
Perrot
Stiles
Cliffords
Girard
Sewel
Beckley
High Street Ferry and Public Land
Colwell
Allen
Blair Mc Clenachan
Syms
Harper Matsey
Crooked Billet Dock
Fox Pryor Howell
Anthony
Pemberton
Chesnut Street Public Landing
Turner Prichard Morris
Pollock Websters
Landenbergs Gilmans
Wilcox
Whartons
Forbes
Walnut Street Public Landing
Kennedys
Ross
Bringhurst Coxs
Morton
Morris
Hamiltons
Public Dock and Landing
Stampers
Spruce Street Public Landing
Walls
Hollingsworth
Syms
Tittermary
Montgomery
Pine Street Public Landing
Wharton Market
Maloney, Nixon
Willings
Willings
Cuthberts
Robins, Cuthbert
Mifflin
Blyth
Cedar Street Public Landing

Cherry Street
Crown
Story Street
Branch Street
Elm Street
Keys Alley
George Alley
Quarry
Bread Street
Elbert Alley
Apple Tree Alley
North Street
South Street
Church Alley
Combes Alley
Tewter Platter A
Minor Street
Sixth Street
Fifth Street
Fourth Street
Third Street
Second Street
Front Street
Water Street
Elbow Lane
White House Alley
Moravian Street
Black House A
Pruant Street
Pear Street
Widinos Alley
Laurel St
Union Street
Gaskill Street
New Market
Dock
Ebb
Ebb

Philadelphia Georgian

Endpapers. A portion of the *Plan of the City of Philadelphia* originally drawn in 1796 by John Hills and engraved in England by John Cooke. This plan, on which surviving structures are indicated in red, is described in Appendix VII, beginning on page 139, and is reproduced by courtesy of the Map Collection of the Yale University Library.

Frontispiece. The Powel House, 244 South Third Street. Built in 1765–66 for Charles Stedman and occupied by Samuel Powel from 1769 until his death in 1793. Although eighteenth-century Philadelphia was noted for the grandeur of its major houses, this is the only example still standing in the old city proper.

Philadelphia Georgian

THE CITY HOUSE OF

Samuel Powel

AND SOME OF ITS EIGHTEENTH-CENTURY NEIGHBORS

BY

GEORGE B. TATUM

WITH PHOTOGRAPHS OF PHILADELPHIA ARCHITECTURE BY

CORTLANDT VAN DYKE HUBBARD

Wesleyan University Press

MIDDLETOWN, CONNECTICUT

1976

The title-page ornament is the crest from the coat of arms on Samuel Powel's bookplate. The Powel arms bore: *Party per fesse, argent and or, a lion rampant gules;* crest: *a star of eight points above a cloud — all proper.* Motto: *Proprium Decus et Patrum* ("My Honor and my Father's"). See also Figure 64.

Library of Congress Cataloging in Publication Data

Tatum, George B.
    Philadelphia Georgian.

    Bibliography: p.
    Includes index.
      1. Philadelphia. Powel House. 2. Architecture, Georgian
— Philadelphia. 3. Architecture, domestic — Philadelphia.
I. Title.
NA707.T37   974.8'11   75-39905
ISBN 0-8195-4095-1
ISBN 0-8195-6044-8 (pbk.)

Manufactured in the United States of America
First edition

To all

who have made possible our enjoyment of the Powel House, but especially

Charles and Ann Stedman, who built it

Samuel and Elizabeth Powel, who improved it

Frances Anne Wister, who led the campaign to preserve it

Contents

List of Illustrations

Acknowledgments

THOUGH HISTORIANS of colonial America have long recognized the signal importance of the Philadelphia house once occupied by the Samuel Powels, many of the questions it invites have remained largely unanswered. How, we should like to know, did the Powels' house compare to others of its time and place? What were the origins of the architectural forms selected and who were the craftsmen employed to execute them? How authentic is the structure we see today? What insight into the values and living patterns of the period does it provide? In search of answers to these and a variety of related questions it has been necessary in the pages that follow to refer to some aspect of nearly every major Philadelphia building that survives from the colonial period. And because architecture is so emphatically a visual art, an effort has been made to match words with photographs, many of them taken by Cortlandt Van Dyke Hubbard specifically for the purpose.

A number of the facts concerning the Powel House were brought to light a decade ago by Nicholas B. Wainwright in the course of his research on the house and furniture of General John Cadwalader. As the first publication of the detailed accounts associated with the decoration and furnishing of a major Philadelphia house in the eighteenth century, Wainwright's *Colonial Grandeur in Philadelphia* was a pioneer work that will be easily recognized as the inspiration for the present study. Thanks are also due its author for numerous specific suggestions and very helpful criticism.

Some of the implications of Wainwright's discoveries were promptly noted by Frederick Hemsley Levis, then president of the Philadelphia Society for the Preservation of Landmarks. It was he who proposed a monograph to commemorate the 200th anniversary of the Powel House, and during the ensuing years, while the author sought to make a place for the project among numerous other duties and responsibilities, this staunch friend of historic preservation continued to provide prompt assistance and patient encouragement.

Members of the board of the Landmarks Society, past and present, also contributed importantly to whatever merit the following discussion of the Powel House may prove to have. First among these are David B. Robb, for many years a bulwark of the society in his role as treasurer, and Mrs. Henry M. Watts, Jr., the able and resourceful chairman of the Powel House Committee, but others helped in a variety of ways. Whitfield J. Bell, Jr., criticized earlier versions of the manuscript and generously made available the unpublished biography he had prepared on Samuel Powel as a member of the American Philosophical Society. Lancelot F. Sims, Jr., A.I.A., not only assisted with the search for solutions to several architectural problems, but also put his own professional skills to redrafting a more accurate plan of the Powel House and three of its important neighbors. The late James Rawle made an extensive survey of secondary sources that provided a valuable supplement to those assembled by the author. Mrs. E. Florens Rivinus offered several helpful suggestions, and the late Calvin S. Hathaway pointed out a number of ways in which the text could, or should, be improved. When he read the manuscript in one of its later drafts, Charles E. Peterson, F.A.I.A., whose own name has long been synonymous with architectural history and preservation in Philadelphia, wisely questioned some of the author's less fortunate assumptions. In his role as photographer, Cortlandt Hubbard generously set a professional fee that took into account very fully his membership on the board of the Landmarks Society.

Notes at the end of the text are intended to acknowledge indebtedness to published sources, but a special word of appreciation is due those students of Philadelphia architecture who shared their specialized knowledge in a variety of ways, especially: Beatrice Kirkbride, whose work for the Philadelphia Historical Commission has made her the surest interpreter of eighteenth-century insurance surveys; Roger Moss, Secretary of the Athenaeum of Philadelphia, who has taken the colonial craftsman in Philadelphia as a subject for investigation; Penelope Hartshorne Batcheler of the National Park Service, whose familiarity with eighteenth-century building practices must surely be unsurpassed; and Margaret B. Tinkcom, for many years historian of the Philadelphia Historical Commission, on whose knowledge of all aspects of eighteenth-century Philadelphia many of us have come to depend. Here, too, should be mentioned Erling H. Pedersen, who generously took time from his architectural practice to recall his role as staff architect and assistant to Fiske Kimball during the time the room from the Powel House was being installed in the Philadelphia Museum of Art. His recollections provided several clues that helped solve the puzzle of exactly how much of the original fabric was available to the restorers of the 1920s.

Carl Bridenbaugh, Robert F. Oaks, Peter Walch, and Charles C. Wall were among others who took time to answer questions that fell within their areas of special competence. William H. White assisted the author in his search of the records of the Philadelphia Society for Promoting Agriculture, as did Edwin Wolf, 2nd, when he sought information relating to Powel's service on the board of the Library Company of Philadelphia. Hamilton Elliott guided a search of the archives of the University of Pennsylvania, and Mrs. Lydia Bond Powel, formerly Keeper of the American Wing of the Metropolitan Museum, not only made available a photograph of the handsome chest of drawers that may once have been in the Powel House, but also supplied valuable information concerning her husband's family. Stuart P. Feld kindly furnished a photograph of Pratt's early portrait of Mrs. Powel while it was at the Hirschl & Adler Galleries.

The good offices of Hannah Benner Roach made it possible to secure the services of Madelene Howland as Quaker genealogist. She not only prevented the author from perpetuating several errors made by others, but also kept him from contributing a number of his own. As archeologist, Barbara Liggett was able to provide vital confirmation of the original form and dimensions of the back building of the Powel House. And despite any inconvenience, Mr. and Mrs. Franklin A. Fleece bore with unfailing good grace many requests to visit the Powel House at odd hours and often with little notice.

The search for material connected with the Powel House led to a number of museums, where members of the staff not only answered inquiries but also helped with the questions. Jay Cantor, then a Chester Dale Fellow, assisted at the Metropolitan Museum of Art, as did John Buchanan, archivist, and Mary Glaze and Morrison H. Heckscher in the American Wing. While Assistant Curator of Decorative Arts at the Philadelphia Museum of Art, Raymond V. Shepherd, Jr., called attention to several important items of furnishing associated with the Powels and assisted with an inspection of the woodwork that the museum had removed from their house on Third Street. Also at the Philadelphia Museum, Beatrice B. Garvan, now Associate Curator of American Art, generously shared pertinent material she had come across in the course of her own research. At the Winterthur Museum, Charles F. Hummel, Curator, and Ian M. G. Quimby, now Editor of Publications, made possible the examination and illustration of the woodwork from the Powel House that had been acquired by the late Henry Francis du Pont. While on the staff at Winterthur, Milo M. Naeve took a lively interest in this study and assisted its author in a variety of ways. At the Newport Historical Society, Elisabeth O. Powel Crosby supplied helpful information concerning Samuel Powel's diary of his trip to the Netherlands, and at the Free Library of Philadelphia the author benefited from the professional assistance and advice of Miriam L. Lesley, Head of the Art Department, when he consulted the measured drawings that comprise the Old Philadelphia Survey.

Every teacher has his own research stimulated and strengthened by that of his students. Some of those who have contributed most directly to this study include: Virginia Burt and Elizabeth Dahill (dining areas); David Crownover (Georgian churches in Philadelphia); Lynne Delehanty DiStefano (Robert Smith); David W. Kiehl (Aesop in Philadelphia); Sarah Lytle (Philadelphia brickwork); Joan Marshall (Philadelphia kitchens); W. John McIntyre (Whitby Hall); Katherine Menz (closets); Ronald Miller (newel posts); Christina Hine Nelson (the Reynolds-Morris house); Gregory Weidman (plaster ceilings); Wendy Wick (the Shippen-Wistar house). Andrew Cosentino and George Gurney kindly took time from busy schedules to help verify facts or trace references. So, too, did David Schuyler, who also pointed out a number of ways in which earlier drafts of the text might be made more complete and accurate.

In common with every student of Philadelphia architecture, the author is indebted to the Philadelphia Contributionship and to the Mutual Assurance Company not only for the care with which they have preserved their insurance surveys, but also for the generosity with which they have made them so readily available to historians. In her role as assistant to Professor Anthony N. B. Garvan in his study of the records of the Mutual Assurance Company, Carol Wojtowicz identified the firemarks appropriate to Samuel Powel's time and obtained the photographs that here serve as tailpieces.

Research of any kind is apt to be expensive. In this case, the Landmarks Society defrayed a substantial part of the cost of photography, and charges for putting the manuscript in final form for publication were met from funds provided its faculty for this purpose by the University of Delaware. To the

Commonwealth Land Title Insurance Company, and to James G. Schmidt and William J. Erwin, Jr., its officers, is owed the detailed brief-of-title that is indispensable for the study of an historic house. And of course without the professional assistance provided by the staff of the Historical Society of Pennsylvania, the investigation of any aspect of Philadelphia's past would be all but impossible.

In recognition of the time and knowledge that many have contributed to this study, it has seemed appropriate to assign any royalties due its author to help insure that the Powel House will still be a source of inspiration and pleasure when Americans gather to celebrate the completion of the third century of their national independence.

G.B.T.

Old Lyme, Connecticut
September 1, 1975

Philadelphia Georgian

PART ONE : THE OWNERS

The Owners

We then visited Mr. Powell, another splendid Seat.

DIARY OF JOHN ADAMS, SEPT. 1, 1774

O F THE MAJOR CITY HOUSES that in the latter half of the eighteenth century helped give to Philadelphia an appearance that Jefferson found "handsomer" than either London or Paris, only the house on the west side of Third Street, midway between Spruce and Walnut, may be said to retain much of its original character.[1] Now numbered 244[2] and known for many years as the "Powel House," this is today owned and maintained for the enjoyment of the public by the Philadelphia Society for the Preservation of Landmarks.

To write of this one house is to touch upon many aspects of life in Philadelphia during the eighteenth century. Here lived rich Samuel Powel (1738–1793), last of the city's colonial mayors and the first to hold that office under the new republic. The Powels were noted hosts in an age notable for its hospitality. No small or simple dwelling would fill their needs, and to provide a setting suitable for the life he envisioned for himself and his bride, Powel embellished his large front chamber with the work of the most talented craftsmen of the day. The results were undoubtedly exceptional, but certainly no more so than the company for which they served as background. Few indeed must have been the Revolutionary leaders who were not at some time guests in this room. The Marquis de Chastellux has left us records of such visits, as has John Adams, and Washington himself probably dined or took tea more frequently at the Powels' than at any other house in Philadelphia outside his own.

The Stedmans

But though Samuel Powel was certainly the most illustrious of its occupants, he was not the first owner of the house that bears his name. That distinction belongs to Charles Stedman (1713–1784), a Scottish ship's master[3] who had prospered in a mercantile partnership formed with his older brother Alexander (1703–1794) shortly after 1746, when the latter is said to have taken up residence in Philadelphia in the wake of the defeat of the Stuart cause at the battle of Culloden. Alexander seems to have read for the bar, but despite the difference in their training, the two Stedman brothers appear to have been remarkably successful in the shop they established on "Second Street almost opposite to Richard Sewell's, Esq."[4] Advertisements that appeared as early as 1749 in *The Pennsylvania Gazette* and elsewhere suggest that the Stedmans dealt principally in dry goods and ship supplies, the latter doubtless a reflection of the training and contacts of the younger brother. Such advertisements also make clear that as agents for ships using the port of Philadelphia, the Stedman brothers received for placement indentured German emigrants from the Palatinate.

Among the new arrivals when the *Nancy* docked in Philadelphia on August 30, 1750, was Heinrich Wilhelm Stiegel,[5] a young man who shortly thereafter anglicized his given names to the "Henry William" by which he has come to be known. Perhaps the Stedmans first met Stiegel in their capacity as agents for the *Nancy*, but however that may be, in 1758 both brothers became partners with him in the ownership of Elizabeth Furnace in Lancaster County, one of the first iron works in that part of Pennsylvania

To the four hundred acres purchased from Jacob Huber — who had not only established Elizabeth Furnace but had also been Stiegel's employer and the father of his first wife — the new owners soon added over ten thousand more. As resident manager of this extensive domain, Stiegel not surprisingly came to be referred to as "Baron" by his tenants and employees, a title that must have seemed even more appropriate after he acquired Tulpehocken Forge in Heidelberg Township about 1760. Renamed Charming Forge, the latter property was soon increased by the ambitious "Baron" until it included over three thousand acres. Stiegel's first partner in Charming Forge was the Lancaster merchant Michael Gross, but he retained his association with the project for only a little more than a year. The importance of this for the story of the Powel House lies in the fact that the purchasers of Gross's interest were the part-owners of Elizabeth Furnace, Charles and Alexander Stedman, who thereby became debtors to Stiegel for about one-third of their half-share, or something more than a thousand pounds.[6]

Not content with even these extensive holdings, on February 17, 1762, the Stedman brothers purchased over seven hundred acres in Rapho Township, Lancaster County, and later the same year conveyed a third undivided interest in this tract to their friend "Baron" Stiegel. In this case it was not iron or wood to smelt it that interested the three partners, but rather the prospect of selling land for settlement. To this they turned at once, paying the surveyor David Stoudt £70 for laying out the streets and surrounding territory of a new town to which they gave the name "Manheim."

But even such diverse business activities as these were not likely to occupy all the time and attention of an ambitious young man in the mobile society of colonial America. In this case Charles's participation in other aspects of urban life was doubtless made more certain by his marriage in Christ Church on January 1, 1748/9, to Ann, daughter of Dr. Thomas Graeme of Graeme Park and granddaughter of Lady Keith, second wife to Sir William Keith, who had served as lieutenant governor of Pennsylvania from 1717 to 1726.[7] At mid-century Philadelphia was developing rapidly, and presumably the newlyweds took an active interest in the establishment of such institutions as the Publick Academy, for which as the College of Philadelphia (now the University of Pennsylvania) Alexander Stedman served continuously as trustee for over two decades, beginning in 1755.[8] In 1752 Charles himself began a term as vestryman of Christ Church that, except for one brief interval, continued for more than twenty-five years. It was during this period that St. Peter's was built at Third and Pine streets as a "chapel of ease" for the parent congregation, a project of which Charles was one of the early supporters.[9] Predictably, the Stedmans were among the original subscribers to the Dancing Assembly in 1748,[10] and the following year when the Scots in Philadelphia commemorated their common origin by the establishment of a charitable organization, Charles helped to found the still-flourishing St. Andrew's Society.[11] The Masons who met at Tun Tavern also counted the younger Stedman brother among their most loyal members,[12] and though never as active in city politics as his older brother, Charles nonetheless served as least one term as Common Councilman.[13]

Possessed of considerable wealth and occupying positions of some prominence in the community, by 1765 both Stedman brothers were ready to have built for themselves fine new houses. The site on the southeast corner of Sixth and High (Market) streets selected by Alexander was at the outer limits of what could then have been considered either a convenient or a fashionable location.[14] Charles, on the other hand, elected to build nearer the Delaware River on the west side of Third Street where he owned a lot purchased five years before from the proprietaries, Thomas and Richard Penn.[15] Extending 396 feet to Fourth Street and abutting on the north the house that William Byrd III had built about 1761,[16] this was clearly a desirable property. Its sixty-foot breadth on Third Street was at least twice that of most residential lots in eighteenth-century Philadelphia. And though from the earliest days of the city larger (i.e. "double") houses had occasionally been built, Charles was following the more usual practice when he limited his to a width sufficient for a single front room with a passage beside it.

But even before his new house (Frontispiece) was entirely finished, Charles's fortunes began to wane. In the spring of 1766 his wife died, and although he remarried in September of the following year,[17] his financial problems persisted. In the first number of *The Pennsylvania Gazette* for 1766, the Stedman brothers referred to their partnership as having already been dissolved, and as his share of the assets Charles began to offer for sale one-third of Elizabeth Furnace, one-quarter of Charming Forge, and one-third of the town of Manheim. Such advertisements continued to appear with some regularity for several years.[18] In the first of them the seller's address is given as Second Street, and no mention is made of his new house, presumably because it was not yet finished. By the fall of 1766, however, advertisements not only described the property on Third Street in some detail but also made it clear that the Stedmans were now living there (*see opposite*).

But buyers for large city houses were apparently not plentiful, and after more than two years Charles was still running the same advertisement with the additional offering of his "new plate," which he was willing to dispose of "at first cost." Not until August 2, 1769, was anyone found to purchase the house on Third Street, and then all of the £3,150 paid went to satisfy the seller's creditors.[19]

The Powels

The buyer of Stedman's house was young Samuel Powel, the third of his family in America to bear that name, who, through the thrift and industry of his Quaker father and grandfather, found himself at an early age the beneficiary of so ample a fortune that, after completing his education at the College of Philadelphia with an extended tour of Europe, he was enabled to divide the remainder of his life between attention to his personal affairs and a career of public service.

From *The Pennsylvania Gazette,* October 16, 1766. The inference that the Powel House was begun in 1765 and finished by the late summer of 1766 is based not only on advertisements such as this but also upon the insurance survey of 1769, which describes the house as then "about 4 years old."

The first of the Powell family in America — the name was then spelled with two "l's" — was another Samuel who, a few months before his death in 1756, recalled that while still a boy he had come to Philadelphia in 1685.[21] His reasons for leaving England were not mentioned, but he appears to have been an orphan and to have come to America in the company of his maternal aunt, Ann Powell Parsons, and of her husband, John, a carpenter from Middlezoy, Somersetshire.[22] The close relationship that continued between Samuel and his aunt and uncle is borne out by the will that John Parsons signed on September 10, 1699, in which he bequeathed to his "wife's kinsman, Samuel Powell" all of his "working Tools and Implements."[23] From this and similar bits of evidence it may be inferred that it was from his uncle that young Powell learned his trade of carpenter, becoming in the process competent beyond the ordinary in the building of bridges.[24]

Like so many other early settlers in Philadelphia, the Parsons were Quakers, and before their nephew could receive an additional £50 under his uncle's will, he had first to choose a wife who met "w'th the approbacon and assent of . . . his aunt & w'th the consent of Fr'ds." Well before his uncle's death in 1705 Samuel did indeed select a wife who had the approval of both Ann Parsons and the Quaker community in general. Dated February 19, 1700/1 and still preserved in the manuscript collection of the Historical Society of Pennsylvania,[25] the marriage certificate of "Samuel Powell of Philadelphia, Carpenter, and Abigail Wilcox, Daughter of Barnabas and Sarah Wilcox, deceased"[26] is chiefly remarkable for the prominence of those who served as witnesses. Both John and Ann Parsons signed, of course, but so did such well-known Quakers as William Penn (in the New World for his second, and last, visit); Hannah Penn, his wife; Edward Shippen (soon to become the first mayor of Philadelphia); Jonathan Dickinson; Nicholas Waln; Edward Pennington; Samuel Carpenter; and David Lloyd. Of the four children born to Samuel and Abigail Wilcox Powell, three lived to maturity: Deborah, who married Joshua Emlen in 1728; Sarah, who in 1730 married Anthony Morris, Jr.; and Samuel, who on November 9, 1732, married his sister-in-law Mary Morris, daughter of Anthony Morris, Sr., a brewer.[27]

Although the first Samuel Powell served at least three terms on the Common Council of his city, he is chiefly remembered by the words of an aged black man who described him to the historian John F. Watson as a "rich carpenter" whose house at the northeast corner of Pine and Second streets stood across from its garden.[28] Too much should not be made of Powell's rise from humble origins to conspicuous riches, however. The aunt and uncle with whom he began life in America apparently occupied respected positions in the community; not only did John Parsons serve on the Common Council in 1704–05, but James Logan, secretary and confidential agent to William Penn, attended his funeral and even thought the event worth reporting to the proprietary himself.[29] Nor should it be supposed that all Powell's wealth came from his own labors. In addition to the previously noted bequests from his uncle, he was also the principal beneficiary of Ann Parsons, who died August 25, 1712.[30] Add to this the fact that his wife had inherited a substantial amount of property before their marriage,[31] and it will be seen that the first Samuel Powell was far from being the entirely self-made man he is sometimes pictured.

And if a rise from obscurity to social prominence in three generations is an oft-told tale in America, it should also be remembered that the later distinction between trades and professions did not exist in eighteenth-century Philadelphia. Not only were there really no professions in the modern sense, but even prominent citizens might list themselves as having a trade, though not actively engaged in it. The most noted of these was of course Benjamin Franklin who, in the familiar preamble to his will, was careful to put his trade of "Printer" ahead of his posts as "Minister Plenipotentiary . . . to the Court of France" and "President of Pennsylvania."[32] As late as 1786, two Samuel Powels (one of them by then deceased) are listed on the roster of members published as part of its *Articles and Rules*[33] by the Carpenters' Company of Philadelphia, an organization of master craftsmen patterned on English models and founded about 1724 for the furtherance of the trade and the care and support of its members, their widows and children. The deceased member was undoubtedly the "rich carpenter," who was one of the earliest members of the company, and it would be tempting (especially in view of the spelling of both names with one "l") to identify the living Powel with the occupant of the fine house on Third Street, who might have taken up membership in the company for sentimental — or possibly political — reasons, though he never earned a shilling at the trade. More likely, the living "Powel" is the "Samuel Powell" who is identified in the published records of the company as having died in 1815 and who would therefore be the one who served as warden in 1771 and who in 1770 took four shares of stock (one of the ten smallest subscriptions) toward the building of the company's new hall.[34]

Samuel Powel, the younger (junior), son of the "rich carpenter," calls himself a "merchant" in his will and is so referred to by others. It was he who is said to have dropped one "l" from the family name, either to avoid confusion with others in the city or to revert to an earlier spelling, though neither he nor many of his contemporaries can be said to have been consistent in this regard. Samuel Powel, Jr., died in 1747 when he was forty-two,[35] nine years before his father, leaving a widow and three children; Abigail, who married William Griffitts; Sarah, who was born the day before her father died and who married Joseph Potts in 1768; and Samuel, the principal subject of this account, who was born October 28, 1738.[36]

As the only male representative of his family, the third Samuel Powel began his adult life with material advantages exceeded by very few young men in colonial America. An heir of his merchant father at the age of nine and a principal beneficiary under the will of his grandfather at eighteen,[37] he received as a matter of course the best education the middle colonies could offer. After preparing at the Academy for two years, in 1756 he entered the College of Philadelphia, from which he was graduated three years later as one of the members of the class of 1759, the second in the history of that institution.[38] From there his path, as that of any young colonial of means, led almost inevitably to Europe.

By opening the Continent to travelers, the Peace of Utrecht (1713) had helped to set the stage for the Grand Tour, which for the remainder of the century — with only wartime interruptions — became an all but indispensable part of the education of the English gentleman. In deciding to visit many of the principal cities of western Europe, Powel was therefore only following the practice adopted by the scions of other prominent Philadelphia families for at least a decade. Rawles, Allens, and Shippens had all preceded him,[39] but what was unusual about his trip was its duration; whereas others had been able or content to travel for a year or two at most, he was abroad from October of 1760 to October of 1767, a total of seven years.

Among other Americans already in England, Powel eventually found his most congenial traveling companion in John Morgan (1735–1789), who had sailed from Philadelphia the preceding May, intent on furthering his medical studies.[40] After spending the summer of 1761 in the Netherlands,[41] Powel was back in London in time for the coronation of George III and later joined Provost Smith and John Inglis of Philadelphia in presenting His Majesty with an address from the College of Philadelphia.[42] Rich, attractive, and well spoken, the young Quaker was so well received wherever he went that there were even those who looked for him to be knighted.

The following summer found Powel touring Scotland in the company of Morgan, who had been studying medicine at Edinburgh. If anything, the Scots impressed the travelers as being even more polite and hospitable than the English, a judgment that seemed confirmed when the Lord Provost and magistrates of Sterling "crowned their uncommon Civilities" by presenting the two Philadelphians with the Freedom of the City. Glasgow, in particular, struck Powel as being not unlike his own city, and when he returned to Scotland the following summer in order to be present when Morgan received his medical degree, both young men were made burgesses and guild brothers of Edinburgh — a signal honor for colonials.[43]

The fall and early winter of 1763–64 were spent in Paris; while Morgan attended lectures and observed hospital practice, Powel took in the sights of the city. It was late February before the two friends started south, and after brief stops at Lyons, Avignon, Nîmes, and Montpellier, they traveled from Antibes to Leghorn by boat, putting in at Genoa on April 1. At Leghorn they were fortunate in being presented to the Duke of York, who promptly extended an invitation to join his party, then on its way to Lucca and Florence. To this they readily agreed, and in the days that followed found themselves included as a matter of course in the entertainments planned in honor of His Royal Highness. In Rome for Holy Week and Easter, the two Protestants from Philadelphia were received with "great Courteousness and Affability" by Pope Clement, who was reported to have asked "many Questions concerning America."[44]

Like other visitors to Rome before and since, Powel was deeply impressed by the ancient ruins he found on every side. "The venerable remains of Antiquity . . . are grand and magnificent beyond what can be conceived by persons who have never seen them," he reported to his friend George Roberts back in Philadelphia.[45] The better to make the most of their opportunities, Powel and Morgan from 10 A.M. to 2 P.M. each day joined several others in a course offered by James Beyers, the antiquarian; and while in Rome both were honored by election to the Accademia degli Arcadi, a society whose members had a common interest in belles lettres. "You see how far our good Fortune surpasses our Merit," Powel wrote enthusiastically to his uncle Samuel Morris.[46]

Before leaving Rome both Morgan and Powel had their portraits painted by Angelica Kauffmann (1741–1807), then at the beginning of a career as one of the most popular painters of her generation. When Morgan refused a fee for prescribing treatment for some minor indisposition, the lovely Angelica offered in return a portrait of herself (Fig. 1), which in due course was delivered to him in London. Some years later, Morgan presented this self-portrait to Powel, who presumably hung it in his house on Third Street; today it is part of the collection of the Pennsylvania Academy of the Fine Arts, to which it was given in 1809 by Mrs. Powel. Powel's own portrait remained in the family, however, and is still owned by one of his wife's collateral descendants (Fig. 2).[47]

"Lolling," as he said, "in the lap of ease," Powel was doubtless tempted to prolong indefinitely a European visit that he admitted to George Roberts had "far exceeded [his] most sanguine expectations." Not until July 6, 1764 — still in the company of Morgan — did he begin the long trip up the Italian peninsula that led back to England and eventually to Philadelphia. But first there were stops to be made at Loretto, Rimini, Bologna, Venice, Padua, and Milan; from Turin the route to Geneva lay across the Alps by way of the difficult Mount Cenis pass.

Once in Switzerland, the two young travelers took time for a call on Voltaire to whom they had been given a letter of introduction by a friend in Rome. Predictably, this part of the tour proved eminently memorable, if not altogether comfortable. The sage of Ferney followed an embarrassingly effusive greeting by trying to draw Powel into a debate on the nature of the soul, and when this failed, he continued with a discussion of the writings of Lord Bolingbroke, which Powel owned with some embarrassment he had never read. Nothing daunted, Voltaire sent his guests on their way with a farewell even more bombastic than his greeting: "Love Truth," he bade them, "hate Hipocrisy, hate Masses, and above all hate the Priests."

Though a birthright Quaker, Powel discovered many of his most congenial friends among the more worldly members of the established church. And so when 1764 found him in London at the same time as Dr. Richard Peters (1704–1776), rector of Christ Church in Philadelphia, it seemed an opportune moment to transfer his allegiance from the Society of Friends to the Church of England, a step his friend Morgan had taken several years before. All was arranged discreetly, and on his return to Philadelphia, Powel proved one of the most active and influential parishioners of Christ Church,

1. Self-Portrait by Angelica Kauffmann. Painted about 1764. Though initially intended for another, this painting in Powel's Philadelphia residence must have daily reminded him of the interesting and important people he had met in the course of a Grand Tour that had kept him in Europe for seven years. Courtesy, The Pennsylvania Academy of the Fine Arts.

2. Portrait of Samuel Powel. Painted by Angelica Kauffmann in 1764. In addition to giving the sitter something to do with his hands, the architectural plan Powel holds may be intended as a reference to the antiquarian studies he had been pursuing while in Rome. Certainly, it does not seem to resemble any known Philadelphia building. Privately owned.

though as a matter of convenience he occupied a pew at St. Peter's, the chapel of ease completed the year after he left on his tour of Europe (Fig. 3).[48]

On August 7, 1769, two years after his return from the Grand Tour, Powel married in Christ Church Elizabeth Willing (1742–1830), one of six daughters of a prominent Philadelphia family and a young woman to whom he was distantly related by marriage.[49] Her father was Charles Willing (1710–1754), a successful merchant who had served as mayor of Philadelphia in 1748 and again in 1754; her mother was Anne Shippen (1710–1791), the granddaughter of Edward Shippen (1639–1712), first mayor of Philadelphia; her brother Thomas (1731–1821), with his partner Robert Morris, would give decisive financial support to the Revolutionary cause and later be elected president of the Bank of North America; her older sister Mary (1740–1814) was the second wife of Colonel William Byrd III (1728–1777), a Virginia gentleman more remarkable for personal charm than for business acumen. At the age of thirty-one, Powel was only five years older than his bride, though there were those who, remembering her earlier interest in others, suggested that at least so far as Elizabeth was concerned "love had not much part in the affair." That, in any case, was the opinion of her grand-nephew Joshua Francis Fisher (1807–1873), but then he was not overly fond of either his great-aunt or of his great-uncle. The fact that Fisher had never known Samuel Powel, who had died fourteen years before he was born, did not prevent him from describing his great-uncle as "rather a conceited priggish man" who made a "precise and peremptory" husband.[50]

The appearance of Elizabeth Willing at the time of her marriage has been preserved in her portrait (Fig. 4) by Matthew Pratt (1734–1805), a young artist just returned to Philadelphia after four years in England. There he had studied for a time with Benjamin West (1738–1820), the first American painter to achieve an international reputation and one whose own studies in Italy Powel had helped to support. The circumstances of Pratt's return in 1768 and of his meeting with several of his future patrons are described in the autobiographical notes he prepared for his son:

[I arrived] May 30th and began my professional line, at the corner of Front & Pine St where I met with my old and good friend, the Revd Thomas Barton of Lancaster, who came purposely to introduce me, to Governor Hamilton, Governor Johnson, Mr. Jno Dickinson, Mr. Saml Powell, and all the Willing family, the Clergy & &c. among whom I met with full employ, for 2 years. . . .[51]

3. Interior of St. Peter's Church, Third and Pine Streets. Erected between 1758 and 1761 by Robert Smith, carpenter-builder. Though located only a few blocks from Christ Church, St. Peter's was preferred by parishioners in the Society Hill area because of the poor condition of Philadelphia streets in the eighteenth century. Today its chief architectural attractions are its original box pews and handsome pulpit at the west end opposite the altar. Both the Charles Stedmans and the Samuel Powels worshipped here.

Prim mouths, full cheeks, and weak chins seem to have been features shared by a number of the women Pratt painted, but if his portrait of Elizabeth Willing was not especially flattering, it appears to have pleased the subject well enough for her to wish to sit for him again in later years. Of course, a painting of a women in her mid-twenties by an artist at the beginning of his career is not necessarily a reliable index of the mature accomplishments of either.

Clearly ability in the Willing family was not confined to the male line; when her husband had so misdirected his affairs that he felt obliged to take his own life, Mary Willing Byrd provided the prudent management that kept its mortgagees from seizing Westover, the Byrd estate in Virginia, with its numerous slaves and rich plate. As testimony that Elizabeth Powel also possessed her share of the talents so notable in other members of her family, we have the comments of the Marquis de Chastellux in the first and privately printed version of his *Travels in North America:*

> . . . contrary to American custom, [Mrs. Powel] plays the leading role in the family — *la prima figura,* as the Italians say. . . . she has not traveled, but she has wit and a good memory, speaks well and talks a great deal; she honored me with her friendship and found me very meritorious because I meritoriously listened to her.[52]

Partly at the urging of Thomas Jefferson, in the later edition of the *Travels* Chastellux softened this and several other remarks about Americans he had met in the course of his sojourn in their country. Nor did Mrs. Powel's loquaciousness deter him from visiting her house on Third Street or prevent his finding there food and conversation so "excellent and agreeable in every respect" that he seems inevitably to have lingered longer than he realized or intended.[53]

Powel's decision to purchase Stedman's new house was clearly predicated on his marriage five days later to Elizabeth Willing, whose brother continued to occupy the family property a few yards to the north, on the southwest corner of what was known, then as now, as Willing's Alley. Certainly Powel himself did not lack for properties that could be occupied as a residence. The first Samuel Powell, the "rich carpenter," is said to have owned ninety houses in the city. To these extensive holdings Powell's son and grandson added others, including the mansion on Second Street built by Edward Shippen and later occupied by several of the colonial governors.[54] This must have been the house that George Roberts referred to in his letter of November, 1763, in which he sought to divert Powel from the attractions of Europe by remarking:

4. Portrait of Elizabeth Willing Powel. Painted by Matthew Pratt in Philadelphia about 1769, and later owned by various members of the Powel family until its acquisition by the Philadelphia Museum of Art. Pratt's portrait may have been intended to mark Elizabeth Willing's marriage to Samuel Powel. Courtesy, Philadelphia Museum of Art, The George W. Elkins Fund, 1973.

. . . your house is so finely situated that it looks like the habitation
of a Turkish Bashaw (the front wall being very high from the street,
occasioned by the late regulations of the pavement) . . . 'tis the
noblest spot in the city — don't you wish to see it?[55]

But though the old Shippen house had been considered good enough for
such governors as Gordon, Thomas, and Denny, its high gambrel roof and
other early features must have seemed badly outdated to the young man but
recently returned from Europe. Nor could Powel and his fiancée have been
wholly indifferent to the fact that the house Stedman was offering for sale
was next to that occupied by Governor John Penn and his lady. By the last
quarter of the eighteenth century the block of Third Street between Spruce
and Walnut had obviously become a fashionable part of town.

In renting the old Shippen mansion from the Powels for use by the
colonial governors, the proprietaries were only following the practice of
most Philadelphians in the eighteenth century, probably not more than
one-fifth of whom owned their own homes.[56] Mention has already been made
of the numerous houses belonging to the first Samuel Powell, and during an
era that knew no banks or public ownership of corporations, real estate —
both inside and outside the city — provided the most common investment
and the principal basis for taxation. It has been estimated from a study of
the 1774 tax list that at that date 10 percent of Philadelphians owned nearly
90 percent of the taxable property,[57] and of these landlords Samuel Powel
may well have been the most notable; at least, his assessment of £1,207
greatly exceeded that of even such rich Philadelphians as Chief Justice
William Allen (£782), the Widow Masters (£683), Thomas Willing (£534),
or John Cadwalader (£143).[58]

Of course during the eighteenth century many forms of wealth went
untaxed, and the only certain fact that can be deduced from comparisons
such as these is that Powel owned more real estate in Philadelphia County
than did any of his contemporaries. But even if he were not the richest
Philadelphian of his day, as is sometimes said, Powel's wealth was obviously
substantial. In the course of a letter introducing him to Thomas Penn in
London, Provost Smith of the College of Philadelphia noted that his former
student controlled a fortune "near £40,000,"[59] and years later Powel's widow
was reputed to be worth £200,000, though details of this kind have a way
of being magnified with the telling.[60]

In addition to a fine house, one of the surest indications of wealth and
social position in the eighteenth century was ownership of a well-appointed
carriage, especially one equipped with four wheels and driven by servants in

5. Powel carriage, now at Mount Vernon. Lighter and less pretentious than the more ponderous "coach," closed carriages with a box for the driver were known as "chariots" in the eighteenth century. This one was exhibited at the Centennial Exhibition of 1876, where it was mistakenly identified as the "White Chariot" in which President Washington made his southern tour in 1791. Courtesy, The Mount Vernon Ladies' Association of the Union.

livery. Those who had this distinction in the Philadelphia of 1772 are known from the list of carriage owners compiled in that year by Pierre Eugène Du Simitière (c. 1736–1784), the Swiss-born historian, artist, and collector of American miscellanea.[61] As Powel's name does not appear among those of the ten owners of a "coach," the largest and most expensive class of carriage, we may assume that his preference for the smaller "chariot" was predicated on considerations other than cost. Like General Washington, he may have desired that his carriages be "handsome, genteel, and light"; at least the Powels are said to have ordered such a vehicle from David and Francis Clark, coach builders of Philadelphia, from whom Washington also purchased a chariot. Restored to its maroon color and blue leather upholstery bordered with lace bearing its original owner's arms, the Powel chariot is today displayed at Mount Vernon as the best available evidence for the type of carriage used by the Washingtons (Fig. 5).[62]

Probably few things would have pleased the Powels more than having their carriage exhibited at Mount Vernon. Fisher's waspish remarks concerning his great-aunt's jealousy toward others in whom Washington took an interest should perhaps not be taken too seriously, but there is no doubt that of Elizabeth Powel's many distinguished guests none was more genuinely welcome than the general. Nor do these sentiments seem to have been entirely one-sided. For a time after Cornwallis' surrender in 1781 the Washingtons took up residence in Philadelphia at the Byrd mansion, and for this and later years, notations in the general's diaries show him to have been a frequent guest next door at the Powels'.[63] One such entry tells of breakfast, followed by a ride to Bartram's garden, which the general found "curious" but "not laid off with much taste." From Bartram's, Washington and Powel rode next to the farm of an otherwise unidentified Mr. Jones where they inspected "the beneficial effects of Plaister of Paris when used in preparing ground for planting." This was on Sunday, June 10, 1787; on August 19 of the same year there was a ride to Whitemarsh, where in the company of Powel the general traversed his "old Incampment, and contemplated on the dangers which threatened the American Army at that place." Understandably, the Washingtons were at pains to repay the hospitality they had received while in Philadelphia; scattered elsewhere in the diaries are records of up to half a dozen visits by the Powels to Mount Vernon.[64] And as even more concrete evidence of his esteem, in 1784 Washington is said[65] to have made Mrs. Powel a present of his portrait by Joseph Wright (1756–1793), which must henceforth have had a place of honor in her house on Third Street (Fig. 6).

Unlike Alexander Stedman and numerous other Philadelphians who remained loyal to the Crown, Powel's sympathies were with the colonists, though his wealth and family background made it all but inevitable that his views on the subject of independence would be moderate. Still in England when Parliament debated repeal of the Stamp Act, he had sought to advance the colonists' cause by paying to have reprinted one of the pamphlets of John Dickinson, the Philadelphian whose writing he had earlier praised for its "noble freedom & manly persuasive eloquence."[66] But when it became clear that there was no further hope of reconciling the differences between the American colonists and the mother country, Powel cast his lot with the revolutionary faction. On May 22, 1778, he took the oath of allegiance to the Commonwealth, and two years later, he subscribed £5,000 toward provisioning the colonial army. Yet despite such actions, it seemed to the Marquis de Chastellux that as late as 1780 Powel's "attachment to the common cause . . . appeared rather equivocal."[67]

6. General Washington. Painted by Joseph Wright in 1784. As developed from his smaller life-study, now also at the Historical Society of Pennsylvania, Wright's painting was acknowledged by the subject as "a good likeness, but not flattering." Later historians have considered it among our most reliable portraits of the first president, however, and the Powels doubtless numbered it among their most valued possessions. Courtesy, The Historical Society of Pennsylvania.

Doubtless the temperate nature of his political views made it all the easier for Powel to preserve a cordial relationship with the Earl of Carlisle during the British occupation of Philadelphia in 1778. As one of His Majesty's commissioners, Carlisle had taken up residence in the main part of the house on Third Street, while its owners were obliged to manage as best they could in the back buildings. On the eve of the British departure his lordship remarked to one of his correspondents on the friendship he had enjoyed with his Philadelphia host by impressment:

> I make him and his wife a visit every day [he wrote], talking politics with them, and we are the best friends in the world. They are very agreeable, sensible people, and you would never be out of their company.[68]

Since Powel presumably knew little of military value, the visits paid him by His Majesty's commissioner have more the character of a courteous exchange between cultivated gentlemen than any kind of treasonable association with the enemy. That, in any case, seems to have been the view of Powel's fellow townsmen, who elected him to the city's highest office both immediately before, and after, the Revolution, a circumstance that later earned him the title of "Patriot Mayor" by which he is sometimes known.[69]

As mayor, Powel was one of the pallbearers at Benjamin Franklin's funeral in 1790, and the largely ceremonial character of many city offices probably led to men of prominence accepting them more as a civic duty than as something to be sought. In the year following his marriage Powel was elected a member of the Common Council,[70] and from that time until his death, except for the period of the Revolution, he served almost continuously in some public capacity: though without formal legal training, he was commissioned a justice of the Common Pleas and Quarter Sessions Courts, April 27, 1772;[71] chosen an alderman two years later, he made the paving of the streets his special concern, a project to which he himself subscribed £50; his service as mayor has already been noted, and after the Revolution he was elected to the Pennsylvania Senate, of which he was made Speaker in 1792, the year before he died.[72]

Shortly before he left on the Grand Tour, Powel had been elected to membership in the "Young Junto," one of several groups of like-minded young Philadelphians who since first brought together by Franklin in 1727 had met intermittently to discuss topics of mutual interest.[73] Absence from the country prevented Powel from attending more than a few meetings, but on his return in 1767 he was invited to take up his membership in the American Society for Promoting Useful Knowledge, to which the Young

Junto had given way. This he did, and in the fall of 1768 found himself
chosen a vice president. In that capacity he assisted in the negotiations that
later resulted in the union of the American Society with the reorganized
American Philosophical Society. His certificate of membership in the new
organization, duly signed by Benjamin Franklin as president, is preserved
at the Historical Society of Pennsylvania,[74] but beyond serving on a committee to procure building materials and making a contribution to the erection
of Philosophical Hall in 1785, Powel took no active part in what was des-
tined to survive as America's oldest learned society.[75]

On balance, Powel cannot be said to have had either a profound or an
original mind; he was at his best in undertakings that called for the active
and practical rather than the intellectual or theoretical. And if naming of
rich men to various boards inevitably raises the question of whether their
selection owed as much to personal ability as to reputed fortune, in this
instance we have the words of Bishop White as testimony to Powel's qualifi-
cations: proposing that he serve as trustee for a Negro school in Philadelphia,
the bishop noted that in addition to integrity, talent, and fortune, his candi-
date had "in a very singular Degree" the further advantage that he was
"Minutely attentive to whatever Business he under[took]."[76]

Powel's term of service as manager both of the Pennsylvania Hospital
(1778–1780)[77] and of the Philadelphia Dispensary (1786)[78] were notably brief.
Nor does he seem to have taken much lasting interest in either the Pennsylvania Society for Promoting Manufactures, for which he served as vice president in 1787, or in the Library Company, to the board of which he was
elected in 1792.[79] His greatest efforts were reserved for his parish, his university, and the Philadelphia Society for Promoting Agriculture, of which he
was one of the founders and the first president.[80]

In the decades immediately following the Revolution the bulk of the
nation's wealth continued to be derived from the land, and the twenty-three
prominent landowners from Philadelphia and the surrounding area who
founded the Agricultural Society sought thereby to bring to American practice some of the scientific advances then to be found in Europe. In this they
were motivated by a sense of patriotic duty as well as by a desire to improve
yields from their own estates. Crop rotation, new varieties of grain, improved livestock, more efficient implements, and the diseases affecting farm
produce were among the topics in which the members of the Agricultural
Society took a particular interest.

Powel's reception into the Anglican fold while in England was noted
earlier, as were his subsequent attendance at St. Peter's and the seriousness
with which he took his duties as churchman. Except for brief periods in 1774

and 1783–84, he served continuously on the vestry of Christ Church from 1773 until his death in 1793.[81] He was a founder, and from 1773 to 1786 treasurer, of the Corporation for the Relief of Widows and Children of Clergymen of the Church of England in America, and when the Episcopal Church was being organized after the Revolution, he was among the Pennsylvania delegates to the convention, held in New York October 6–7, 1784. The following May he was again a lay member of the convention and in that capacity signed the "Plan for Obtaining Consecration" of the American bishops.[82] And if Powel's election as a trustee of the College of Philadelphia in 1773 came in the wake of a generous contribution to that institution,[83] in the years that followed he served faithfully and effectively as a member of various committees and in 1778–79 as treasurer.[84] Indeed, of the usual satisfactions of life, only children seem to have been denied him; his two sons — both named for their father — died in infancy.[85]

In the eighteenth century nearly every Philadelphian of consequence had a summer residence outside the city. To that end, on November 13, 1775, the Powels paid £1,675 to Thomas Willing, Tench Francis, and their respective wives for ninety-seven acres on the west bank of the Schuylkill River, but probably the troubled times that attended the outbreak of the Revolution prevented the development of "Powelton" as its owners would have wished.[86] Little is known of the house said to have been erected about 1779; presumably it was comparatively simple and perhaps nothing more than the "small farmhouse" to which Powel was taken when he contracted yellow fever during the epidemic of 1793. There on September 29, he died, attended by his black coachman and Dr. Samuel Powel Griffitts, his sister Abigail's son who had become a physician.[87] The hero of the time was Dr. Benjamin Rush (1746–1813), who also visited Powel during his last illness, but whose method of treatment, which involved extensive purging and bleeding, was so severe that it was probably more dangerous than the fever and hardly less unpleasant.[88] The stone that marks Powel's grave is still to be seen, beside that of his wife and two infant sons, in Christ Church burying ground at Fifth and Arch streets. Weathering has rendered illegible the lengthy inscription that read in part:

> He was the enemy of all exorbitant Powers / and a sincere friend to the Liberties of his Country. / To all this was added a Taste for Science, for the Fine Arts / and for all the Improvements of Civil Life.[89]

The same year that saw the end of Powel's life was also that in which his wife marked her fiftieth birthday. It was perhaps in celebration of the latter event that Matthew Pratt again painted Elizabeth Willing Powel, by then the poised matron who looks forth from the canvas in the Pennsylvania Academy of the Fine Arts (Fig. 7). [90] Now with no hope of children of her own, shortly after her husband's death Mrs. Powel adopted as her heir the youngest son of her sister Margaret (1753–1816), John Powel Hare who in appreciation changed his name to John Hare Powel on reaching his majority in 1807.[91]

Though an attractive woman and possessed of one of the largest fortunes in the city, Elizabeth Powel lived out as a widow the thirty-seven years of life remaining to her. She is said to have rarely appeared in public and to have spent more and more time at her country seat across the Schuylkill. There about 1800 she began the fine mansion pictured in the well-known water color by David J. Kennedy.[92] Though the house and what remained of the garden were destroyed in 1885, the general location of Powelton is still marked by the avenue and section in West Philadelphia that bear its name.

Later Owners

Perhaps the house to which she had come as a bride held too painful memories or perhaps she simply preferred a different location[93]; whatever the reason, on November 26, 1798 — five years after her husband's death — Powel's widow sold the house on Third Street to William Bingham, the rich banker who had married her niece Anne and who ten years before had built the finest house in the city on the property immediately to the south (Fig. 8).[94] A year later, Bingham gave the Powel House to his daughter Ann Louisa,[95] who on August 23, 1798, had married Alexander Baring, later the first Baron Ashburton. Here were born their two sons before the house was sold, on February 8, 1805, to William Rawle, a prominent attorney.[96]

In May of 1825, Rawle sold off the south portion of the lot on which Samuel Powel had made his garden,[97] so that when the New York attorney Charles Wilkes bought the house on May 19, 1828, the lot was reduced to 30 by 180 feet.[98] From Wilkes, the Powel House passed (April 20, 1829) to the Philadelphia merchant Isaiah Hacker,[99] and from his estate, in turn, to L. Theodore Salaignac, a lawyer (January 19, 1886)[100] and to Wolf Klebansky (December 29, 1904).[101]

Klebansky's means of livelihood is best described in the words of his business letterhead:

Importer, Exporter and Jobber of All Kinds of Russian and Siberian Horse Hair and Bristles — Manes and all Kinds of Animal Hair

7. Portrait of Mrs. Samuel Powel. Painted by Matthew Pratt about 1793. Though the sitter wears a light yellow dress instead of the traditional black of mourning, the word "Farewell," visible in part on the urn in the background, has suggested to some that this portrait should be associated with Samuel Powel's death. Courtesy, The Pennsylvania Academy of the Fine Arts.

8. Third Street looking northwest from Spruce. Plate 18 in the first edition of William Birch's *The City of Philadelphia . . .* , published in 1800. The Bingham mansion is in the foreground, and the Powel House may be seen in the middle distance. Perhaps significantly, neither is shown as having exterior shutters. At the time of their publication Birch's engravings represented the handsomest and most extensive series available for any American city. Courtesy, Kean Archives, Philadelphia.

> Supplied to the Curled Hair Trade — Also Manufacturer of Drawn
> Hair for the Supply of Brush Manufacturers and Hair Cloth
> Weavers.[102]

In pursuit of his somewhat unusual occupation, Klebansky apparently lived with his wife in the house that had been built immediately to the south (now demolished for the present garden), while conducting his business in the Powels' former residence and in certain structures he had erected to the rear.

Since Georgian woodwork contributed nothing to the wholesale hair trade, Klebansky seems to have been glad enough to sell the interiors of the two principal rooms on the second floor of the Powel House. As the best preserved, that in the rear was acquired in 1917 by the Metropolitan Museum of Art, then in the process of establishing its now-famous American Wing.[103] What remained of the upstairs front room was purchased in 1925 by the Pennsylvania Museum and School of Industrial Art (since April of 1938, the Philadelphia Museum of Art) as one of the major installations it hoped to make in its new building, which by that time was taking shape on the height of Fairmount at the northwest end of the Benjamin Franklin Parkway.[104] Later the same year the Klebanskys gave the Philadelphia Museum all the remaining woodwork of importance, except for the fine mahogany stair, which as long as the house stood was needed for access to the second and third floors.[105] Though obviously in need of funds, the Klebanskys appear to have been genuinely concerned that the interiors of the Powel House be preserved and that insofar as possible they be kept in Philadelphia.

The Great Depression that brought financial distress to many seems also to have involved Wolf Klebansky, by then a widower, who early in 1931 proposed to sell his property on Third Street to make way for an "open-air garage."[106] On learning of the impending destruction of the Powel House — now little more than a shell, to be sure — a few interested persons put up $1,000 to take an option and halt demolition. In the course of a subsequent meeting at the headquarters of the Colonial Dames on February 27, an enlarged group of concerned citizens under the effective leadership of Miss Frances Wister determined to form an organization that could seek additional funds for what was clearly becoming an ambitious project. In this way the Philadelphia Society for the Preservation of Landmarks came into being, and during the decade that followed, through the energy and devotion of Miss Wister and her associates, the house on Third Street was gradually restored to something approaching its appearance in the days of Samuel Powel.[107]

Indeed, so successful was the Landmarks Society in restoring the Powel House that its members were emboldened to consider similar projects elsewhere. In 1940 they took title to the large stone house in Germantown that John Wister (d. 1789) had built in 1744 as a summer residence. Known since the middle of the nineteenth century as "Grumblethorpe," Wister's "Big House" has been gradually stripped of its later accretions, and its fine garden replanted.

Through the generosity of the Annenberg Fund, in 1965 the Landmarks Society was also given the house (Fig. 9) located a block to the west of the Powel House on Fourth Street that was once the residence of the noted Philadelphia physician with the peculiarly apt name of Philip Syng Physick (1768–1835). On the ground floor, especially, some of the interiors of Physick's house had been altered in the 1850s or later damaged beyond recovery,

9. Hill-Physick-Keith House, 321 South Fourth Street. Built in 1786 for Henry Hill (1732–1798), a prosperous wine merchant. The flatter surfaces and more delicate details of post-Revolutionary houses contrast sharply with the bolder forms of such Middle Georgian predecessors as the Powel House. Nowhere do these later characteristics appear to better advantage than in the graceful doorways with slender sidelights and large fan-shaped transoms that figure so prominently on the facades of houses such as this one. To the right may be seen the tower and spire that William Strickland (1788–1854) added to St. Peter's Church in 1842. Now a property of the Philadelphia Society for the Preservation of Landmarks.

and these were replaced by new details in keeping with the well-preserved exterior.[108] Shortly thereafter, a grant from the Benjamin Franklin Foundation made it possible to recreate the garden, using forms and plant materials popular in the early nineteenth century. As the only example of a major residence of the Federal period still standing in the old section of Philadelphia, the Hill-Physick-Keith House will be encountered again in the course of the general discussion of Georgian architecture that follows.

Philadelphia Georgian

PART TWO : THE FABRIC

The Fabric

Philadelphia Georgian

WHEN THE Stedman brothers began their houses, the architectural style prevailing in Philadelphia — and with local variations throughout the English-speaking world — was the distinctive adaptation of Italian Renaissance forms historians have found convenient to call "Georgian" in recognition of its having reached fullest and most characteristic development during the reigns of the first three monarchs of the Hanoverian dynasty (1714–1820).[1]

Early Georgian in America (c. 1700–c. 1750). A renewed appreciation of Roman classicism had begun in Italy as early as the fifteenth century, of course, and the use of the term "Georgian" should not be understood to imply that there had been no English interest in the antique prior to 1714 and the accession of George I. But since the break with Rome during the reign of Henry VIII (1509–1547) had reduced direct contacts with Italy to a minimum, the whimsical classicism that prevailed during the reigns of Elizabeth I (1558–1603) and James I (1603–1625) had usually been borrowed at second hand from France and Flanders. And though later, for his designs at Whitehall and Greenwich, Inigo Jones (1573–1652) had gone directly to Italian models and to Andrea Palladio (1518–1580), their most popular and intelligible exponent, the development of a full-fledged Renaissance style in English architecture was obliged to wait the passing of the unsettled conditions that attended the Puritan Revolution and the Interregnum (1649–1660) that accompanied it.

When at last the Restoration under Charles II (reigned 1660–1685) brought the arts again into favor, the prevalence of more complicated and dramatic designs indicate that architects like Sir Christopher Wren (1662–1723) and Sir John Vanbrugh (1664–1726) were looking for inspiration to post-Palladian models of seventeenth-century (Baroque) Italy, while the frequent use of red brick set off with trim of light stone we associate with Wren and his followers is a reminder of England's close cultural ties with Protestant and democratic Holland — ties made even closer in 1689 when Parliament invited William, Prince of Orange, to join his wife Mary (1662–1694) on the English throne as William III (d. 1702).

Though it is by no means certain that Wren had a direct hand in the design of any of the buildings at Williamsburg, Virginia, and elsewhere throughout the colonies sometimes attributed to him,[2] his influence may undoubtedly be seen in their style, as in that of such other early colonial structures as Richard Munday's Colony House (1739) at Newport, Rhode Island, the Second Town-House (1712) in Boston, or Philadelphia's State House (Independence Hall), begun in 1732.[3] As befits a leading architectural expression of traditional Christianity, Christ Church[4] is unusual even for Philadelphia in the richness and variety of its decoration (Fig. 10), but with a few exceptions such as this, most buildings erected in America during the first half of the eighteenth century were characterized by exteriors of notable simplicity.

This must have been true of even the most important Philadelphia houses of the period, and though none of these survives in the old part of the city, we may be helped in visualizing their appearance by the small house (Fig. 11) that in the late nineteenth century was moved from its original site near the Delaware River to Fairmount Park in the belief it had been occupied by William Penn. Though its only connection with Penn was its location on land he had once owned and on a court named for his daughter, the house does seem to have been built about 1713 and therefore serves as a useful reminder of the general simplicity that marked most colonial buildings of the Early Georgian period.

Predictably, country houses have fared better than those in Philadelphia itself. To the south, in what was originally farmland along the Schuylkill River, there is Bellaire, with its restored balcony and important early paneling, while north of the old city, in Whitemarsh Valley, one may still visit Hope Lodge, now a property of the Commonwealth of Pennsylvania and a house that seems to have been built sometime before 1741. But perhaps most important, in Germantown the fine "plantation house" of James Logan

10. Christ Church, Second Street north of Market. Rebuilding begun in 1727; tower completed in 1754. John Kearsley, a prominent physician, represented the parish in the construction of the church and is believed to deserve much of the credit for its design. Except possibly for St. Philip's in Charleston, S. C. (begun 1710; burned 1835), Christ Church appears to have been the most ambitious Early Georgian church erected in the colonies. The Venetian (Palladian) window at the east end would not become common in American architecture before the middle of the eighteenth century.

11. Letitia Street House. Built on Letitia Street (Court) near the Delaware River about 1713; moved to Fairmount Park in 1883. The full curves of the brackets that support the flat hood over the doorway are perhaps indicative of the Baroque influences most noticeable in the colonies during the first half of the eighteenth century. The cove cornice is an English feature widely used by early builders in Pennsylvania and New Jersey, but the dormer appears to be a later addition. Many houses of this kind must once have stood in the old section of the city. Now in the custody of the Philadelphia Museum of Art.

(1674–1751), friend and confidant of the Penn family, has survived into the twentieth century virtually unaltered (Fig. 12).[5]

12. Stenton, Germantown. Built between 1723 and 1730. The hipped roof, the simple doorway with its triangular transom, and the flattened brick arches above openings at the lower levels are all features that are duplicated with minor variations in numerous Early Georgian buildings throughout the English colonies. A growing concern with the classical canons of taste that distinguishes the Renaissance approach to architecture may be seen in the symmetrical spacing of doors and windows, in the modillioned cornice at the eaves, and in the incipient pilasters that mark the principal divisions of the facade and define its limits. Now in the custody of the National Society of the Colonial Dames of America in the Commonwealth of Pennsylvania.

Middle Georgian in America (c. 1750–c. 1780). Except for the ubiquitous cornice decorated with modillions (brackets), a few quoins (blocks) to mark the corners, and an occasional timid pilaster, not until the middle of the eighteenth century did classical elements begin to appear in quantity on the exterior of American buildings, and then they were usually handled with a severity and restraint based on the return to Palladian principles that had taken place in England under the leadership of the third Earl of Burlington (1695–1753) and such prominent members of his circle as Colen Campbell (1676?–1729) and William Kent (1684–1748). This neo-Palladian or Middle Georgian phase of American architecture is conveniently dated between the middle of the century and the Revolution and, so far as Philadelphia is concerned, may be said to have begun with Edmund Woolley's tower for the State House (1750–53; wooden steeple rebuilt in 1828 from designs by William Strickland).

Consistent with the principle that new architectural forms tend to appear on the interior, more or less complex classical elements had been used with some frequency in American halls and parlors since early in the eighteenth century. A similar practice continued throughout the Middle Georgian period, though usually with evidence of a surer grasp of Renaissance style on the part of the designer. Doubtless this reflected not only improved training of the craftsmen who were immigrating to the colonies but also greater use of the English architectural books that began appearing in considerable numbers after 1715, the year that saw the publication of the first complete English edition of Palladio. Though owing little or nothing to Palladio, more attention was now given to stairways, while mantels, cornices, and the like were often elaborately carved in a manner that reflected forms earlier made popular in England by the talented and fashionable carver Grinling Gibbons (1648–1721). Principal rooms might still be fully wainscoted, but with increasing frequency paneling was confined to the chimney breast and the area below the chair-rail.

To this period belong such civic or quasi-public structures as the east portion of the Pennsylvania Hospital (cornerstone laid 1755) at Eighth and Pine streets,[6] and the headquarters of the Carpenters' Company (begun 1770), which now seems somewhat lost without the surrounding structures that formed the court in which it originally stood (Fig. 20).[7] Mount Pleasant (Fig. 13) and Woodford (begun c. 1759; additions 1772),[8] both open to the public in Fairmount Park, and Cliveden in Germantown (Fig 14), now a property of the National Trust,[9] are the extant country seats that parallel Charles Stedman's town house on Third Street and together with it represent the best domestic examples of the Middle Georgian style in the Philadelphia area.[10]

13. Mount Pleasant, Fairmount Park. Later called by John Adams "the most elegant seat in Pennsylvania," this impressive country house had been begun in 1761 for Captain John Macpherson (d. 1792), a colorful Scot who had amassed a considerable fortune while serving as a privateer during England's conflict with France and Spain. The projecting central section, the Palladian window, and the doorway ornamented with the columns and entablature of the Doric order are all part of the greater elaboration that characterizes buildings of the Middle Georgian period. Less typical is the omission of covered passageways, which by the middle of the eighteenth century had been found to be a convenient way to link the flanking outbuildings to the main block. In 1779 Benedict Arnold bought Mount Pleasant for his bride, the vivacious Peggy Shippen of Philadelphia, but his subsequent treason prevented him or his wife from ever occupying it. Now in the custody of the Philadelphia Museum of Art.

14. Cliveden, Germantown. Begun in 1763 for Attorney General Benjamin Chew (1722–1810). The gray stone was a local material favored in the Germantown area, but the urns on the roof were imported from England and a detail more often found on public buildings than on private ones. With the help of friends, the owner may have worked out the general design of Cliveden, though the details and their execution were necessarily entrusted to local craftsmen like the master-carpenter Jacob Knor. Now a property of the National Trust for Historic Preservation.

Late Georgian in America (c. 1780–c. 1800). Although Palladio made the mistake of supposing that the exteriors of Roman houses resembled those of public buildings, free-standing temple porticoes were rare in America — and apparently nonexistent in Philadelphia — prior to the Revolution.[11] Not until the late 1780s did William Hamilton add such a feature to The Woodlands, (Fig. 15), his country mansion west of the Schuylkill, and on public buildings the free-standing giant order seems to have appeared earliest in Philadelphia on the First Presbyterian Church on Market Street (built 1793–

15. The Woodlands, West Philadelphia. Begun about 1742 for Andrew Hamilton, II, and remodeled (or rebuilt) about 1788 for his son William (1745–1813). In the eighteenth century its giant portico provided residents of The Woodlands a superb view of the Schuylkill River. Especially on the land side, shown here, the use of giant pilasters also recalls the work of the Brothers Adam in England, and the sophistication with which curvilinear forms are handled throughout the design goes so far beyond anything being attempted by contemporary American builders as to suggest that Hamilton may have brought from London the plans for his new house. In 1845 the mansion and several acres of surrounding land were acquired for use as a cemetery, a function they still serve.

94; demolished c. 1825) and on the Bank of the United States (Fig. 16) begun in 1795 two blocks north of the Powel House from the designs of
Samuel Blodget, Jr., a gentleman-architect and entrepreneur of sorts.[12] But
most characteristic of the final phase of the Georgian style is the increasing
flatness, greater attenuation, and marked delicacy with which the Renaissance vocabulary of Roman architectural forms is handled. Such qualities
are indicative of the greater sophistication that not infrequently attends the
last phase of any style, but in the case of Georgian architecture they were
reinforced by the discovery of Roman frescoes in the excavation of Pompeii
and Herculaneum, works of art that were themselves a late manifestation of
classical culture.

Though they are well illustrated by the Center House (Fig. 17) at the
Pennsylvania Hospital[13] or by William Thornton's winning design for the
building of the Library Company (1789; original demolished 1885),[14] the
distinctive qualities of the Late Georgian style are better suited to domestic
structures than to the larger scale of public ones. The house patterned on
that of the Duke of Manchester that William Bingham built in 1785–86[15]
on the property adjoining the Powel House to the south was noted earlier
when it was called probably the finest American house of its day (Fig. 8).
After being damaged by fire and serving as a hotel for many years, what remained of the Bingham mansion was finally demolished in the mid-nineteenth century, but a few other Late Georgian houses remain as evidence
of Philadelphia's contribution to the domestic architecture of the period.
The only example of note in the old city proper is the house on Fourth
Street, once occupied by Dr. Philip Syng Physick and mentioned previously
as one of the properties of the Landmarks Society (Fig. 9), but of the examples outside the eighteenth-century city, The Woodlands (Fig. 15) has already been noted, and in Fairmount Park are Lemon Hill (Fig. 18),[16] Sweetbrier (1797), Rockland (c. 1800), and The Solitude (1785), the latter now in
the Zoological Gardens.

Insurance Surveys

By modern standards, the Philadelphia to which Powel returned in 1767 was
comparatively small and mean. Even in the more populated sections of the
city, many streets were unpaved and poorly lighted, and safety of life and
property was largely a matter of private initiative. As one moved westward
from the Delaware River, houses became increasingly scattered beyond Sixth
Street, and indeed the total population of the city proper was probably under seventeen thousand.[17] Modern zoning practices whereby the city is divided into separate residential and commercial areas were of course un-

16. First Bank of the United States, South Third Street. Built in 1795–97 from designs of Samuel Blodget, Jr. (1757–1814). National independence did not mean a corresponding break in the Georgian tradition for American buildings. The temple portico was new for Philadelphia, but the close resemblance of the First Bank to a large house serves as a reminder that domestic models continued to dominate American architecture as they had throughout the eighteenth century. Now a part of the Independence National Historical Park.

known; many merchants conducted business from their own houses, and any grouping by trade or occupation was in great part the result of chance or convenience. The fact that in Powel's day the area of Third Street where he lived remained entirely residential was largely a coincidence. Many city blocks had at least one stable, and a variety of more or less offensive odors bore witness to inadequate sanitary facilities.

But of all the hazards to which the city dweller was prey throughout the eighteenth century, none was more common or more to be feared than the ever-present danger of fire. Predictably, Benjamin Franklin was among those who organized the first fire brigade in Philadelphia and one of the first in the colonies. That was in 1736, and in 1752 Franklin helped to form the Philadelphia Contributionship for the Insurance of Houses from Loss by Fire, a company that patterned its practices on those that had grown up in England in the wake of the Great Fire of 1666.[18] The first insurance was written for a term of seven years, but after 1809–10 it became customary to issue policies that were "unlimited" (i.e. perpetual), a practice that continues today. To mark those houses it had insured, the Contributionship — to use the short title by which it is usually known — placed on each a small wooden plaque on which was mounted a reproduction in lead of four hands clasped to form a square, the so-called fireman's carry and a symbol of solidarity based on mutual assistance that inevitably gave rise to the popular nickname "Hand-in-Hand." As in the case of so many Philadelphia institutions, the Contributionship has survived to the present day, when the surveys in its files have proved of inestimable value to the historian.

Like any prudent householder, Powel made it a practice to insure his properties. Within a month of his purchase of Stedman's house he applied for and received insurance totaling £1,500 (£1,000 on the house and £500 on the back building) based on a survey included here as Appendix I. Summary as this is, it nonetheless represents our earliest description of the house on Third Street, aside from the details published in Stedman's advertisement for its sale.

To the managers of the Contributionship it had appeared almost from the outset that any trees in the proximity of one of their insured properties offered an unnecessary hazard. The outbreak of the Revolution deterred them from acting on this premise, but after hostilities ended and the city had begun to return to its former ways, they declined to accept risks of this kind, and in 1784 the Mutual Assurance Company was formed for this purpose, with Powel among its promoters. Appropriately, the new company took as its firemark a small tree cast in lead and mounted on a wooden plaque.

"Two small Trees before the Door and several in the Garden" put

17. Center House, Pennsylvania Hospital, Pine Street between Eighth and Ninth. Built between 1794 and 1805, probably from designs of David Evans, Jr. The Pennsylvania Hospital was planned shortly after 1750 as the first major structure in the American colonies intended specifically for medical purposes, but despite the support of Franklin and others, it took more than half a century to complete the building. When finally constructed, the second story of the center house contained the country's first clinical amphitheater. The light and graceful proportions of the exterior made it a notable example of the Late Georgian style.

Powel's house in the category of those the Contributionship would no longer insure, and his new policy for a total of £1,800 with the "Green Tree" (as the Mutual Assurance Company is familiarly known) is dated January 11, 1785. When considered in the light of the earlier survey by the Contributionship and the entries in his ledger, this second survey (Appendix I) offers useful clues pointing to the changes Powel made in the Third Street house after its purchase from Stedman in the fall of 1769. Too much should not be made of small differences between the two surveys, of course; not only were they made by different men, but each was probably worked up at the surveyor's home or place of business from notes made earlier on the site.

These two surveys — one of 1769 and the other of 1785 — are the only ones bearing directly on the eighteenth-century appearance of Powel's house that have thus far come to light. Yet, when put against their earlier counterparts, the more detailed descriptions characteristic of surveys made in the nineteenth century often provide valuable information even for the historian interested primarily in Georgian buildings. On that basis the survey made by the Contributionship for Isaiah Hacker on May 14, 1859, is included as Appendix II. This should prove helpful for a variety of reasons but particularly for the plan of the ground floor it contains.

Powel's association with both the Contributionship and the Mutual Assurance Company is recalled by the modern replacements of the firemarks of both these companies that have been hung below the upper-story windows of his restored house on Third Street (Frontispiece). With the establishment of the first City Fire Department in 1871, such devices became largely decorative. Prior to that time, however, they served to elicit aid from others insured in the same fashion and to put the volunteer fire brigades on notice that a blaze promptly and efficiently extinguished could be expected to bring a reward from the company whose firemark the house bore. Originally, policy holders were expected to see to it that their houses were identified by the proper firemark, but by the time Powel purchased his house, the Contributionship had found it expedient to assume this responsibility.

Craftsmen

Perhaps his financial reverses prevented Stedman from finishing his house, or at least from finishing it as handsomely as he might have wished. In any case, it does not seem to have entirely satisfied the Powels, who began a number of additions as soon as they secured possession. Such alterations by new owners have probably been common in every age; for eighteenth-century Philadelphia we have the most complete documentation for the changes made by General John Cadwalader to the dwelling on Second Street he had

18. Lemon Hill, Fairmount Park. Built or remodeled about 1800 for Henry Pratt (d. 1838), a Philadelphia merchant; restored in 1926 by Fiske Kimball. Historians are uncertain if any of the present fabric is part of The Hills, the country estate sold by the sheriff in 1799 to satisfy the debts of Robert Morris (d. 1806), "financier of the Revolution." Certainly the curvilinear forms that so interested Late Georgian builders were rarely used to better effect than in the large semicircular bay seen here. Now in the custody of the Colonial Dames of America, Chapter II.

purchased from Samuel Rhoads just a month before the Powels acquired their new house a block to the northwest. As carefully analyzed by Nicholas B. Wainwright and handsomely published by the Historical Society of Pennsylvania,[19] the Cadwalader accounts expand importantly our knowledge of Philadelphia building practices at mid-century.

For assistance with the alterations he proposed to make, there was no one upon whom Powel could rely as architect, at least in the modern sense of someone specifically trained to make his living by designing structures for others to erect. Throughout the eighteenth century, in Philadelphia, as elsewhere in America, important buildings usually began as a general concept originated by some gentleman-amateur — or by a group of such persons functioning as a building committee — which was then executed in detail by competent local craftsmen, one of whom occasionally undertook the general direction of the whole project. When such an "undertaker" was employed, he usually agreed in advance to erect either the complete building or a portion of it for a specified sum, as does the modern builder; more frequently, however, the client paid individual workmen on the basis of time spent or work accomplished. The latter practice seems to be that most often followed in Philadelphia and helps to explain why the Carpenters' Company guarded so jealously the copies of its *Articles and Rules,* a small volume mentioned earlier,[20] that, in addition to illustrating the basic Georgian architectural vocabulary, gave directions and prices for determining "by measure" the cost of completed work. This may also have been the method preferred by Powel, but "for finishing a room" he did make a "Contract" with Robert Smith (c. 1722–1777), the carpenter-builder whom he had earlier engaged to build two houses on Second Street, presumably intended as investments. The £268 that Smith charged would indicate substantial additions to the house as sold by Stedman, and to that sum was later added £49 19s. 3d. for still other "Alterations in said House" (Fig. 19).

To work by contract required, of course, that the builder have sufficient capital to pay his workmen until construction — or at least a portion of it — had been completed, and the man whom Powel selected was the most prominent and successful Philadelphian then engaged in this type of work. It is entirely likely, in fact, that the Stedman brothers may earlier have employed Smith for one or both of their houses. Not only was he among the builders best qualified for an undertaking of that scope and importance, but as an emigrant from Scotland, he was undoubtedly well known to the Stedmans through their common membership in the St. Andrew's Society.

Not a great deal is known about Smith's personal life, but from numerous scattered references it is possible to piece together the general outlines of

Robert Smith

17 9				
June 22	To Cash paid him	£150		
July 22	To Do	64		
August 4	To Do	103		
5	To Do	32		
17	To Do	102		
September 7	To Do	100		
October 9	To Do	66		
	To Do	50		
Novemb 25	To Do	40		
Decem 16	To Do	15		
26	To Do	82		
1769 January 20	To Do	30		
March 11	To Do	52	5	6
April 11	To Do	60		
25	To Do	14		
May 20	To Do	20		
31	To Do	56		
June 21	To Do	280		
August 15	To Do	200		
16	To Do	100		
Septem 22	To Do	35		
October 11	To Do	40		
27	To Do	15		
	To Do by withdrawing an Action against Fenwick	16		
Novemb 10	To Do	15		
Decem 5	To Do	30		
16	To Do	15		
1770 January 12	To Do	53		
26	To Do	39		
February 5	To Do	40		
27	To Do	18		
March 9	To Do	50		
May 4	To Do	10		
22	To Do	30		
June 22	To Do	21		
October 19	To Do	21		
Novemb 3	To Do	6		
12	To Do	100		
1771 January 9	To Do	6		
March 1	To Do	9		
18	To Do	16		
29	To Do	21		
April 12	To Do	10	5	
29	To Do	27		
May 17	To Do	9		
July 15	To Do	3	4	5
Augt 31	To Do	441	13	6
	To a Lott in second Street sold him	100		
1773 April 22	To Cash paid him	100		
June 1	To Do	53		
Septem 10	To Do	25		
Nov 16	To Do	21		
Decemr 15	To Do	82		
1774 January 24	To Do	9		
1776 January 5	To Do	13		
1771 February 9	To 21½ Cords of Wood delivered to his Order	5	12	6
	To 54 white Oak posts omitted			

By his Contract for building two Houses in Second Street	£1000		
By his Contract for an additional Building to one of said Houses	373		
By his Account for additional Finishings to said Houses	56	5	6
By his Contract for finishing a Room in his dwelling House	260		
By his Account for Alterations in said House	49	19	3
By Do for Repairs at sundry Places	15	7	2
By his Contract for building Stores	382		
By his Contract for raising Stores	132		

See Folio

19. Account of Robert Smith in Samuel Powel's ledger. From this it appears that although Smith made it a practice to do Powel's work at a price contracted for in advance, he also received regular monthly payments as the work progressed. The first three entries in the right column have to do with houses Powel was having built as investments, but entries four and five refer to his own "dwelling House" on Third Street. Courtesy, The Historical Society of Pennsylvania.

his career.[21] Early in 1750 we meet him as "House Carpenter" for alterations in the building on Fourth Street below Arch that the trustees of the newly formed Academy of Philadelphia had just acquired from the followers of the popular evangelist George Whitefield;[22] and later that same year, he is listed as one of several carpenters for the important Second Presbyterian Church that stood until its demolition in the nineteenth century at Third and Arch streets. Work on the Second Presbyterian Church apparently occupied Smith for two years, and this was followed by employment between 1752 and 1754 as principal carpenter for construction of the steeple of Christ Church (Fig. 10), which must have been among the highest structures in the colonies at the time of its completion. During these years the surrounding areas often looked to Philadelphia for their craftsmen, and between 1754 and 1756 Smith was occupied with the building of Princeton's Nassau Hall, the design of which he seems to have developed in collaboration with Dr. William Shippen, brother of a trustee of the College of New Jersey (as Princeton University was then known) and the man who played the role of "gentleman-amateur" in this case.[23]

As "City house carpenter," from 1758 to 1761 Smith was in charge of the construction of St. Peter's, noted earlier for its association with both the Stedmans and the Powels (Fig. 3). During its later phases this project may not have claimed all Smith's time, however, for in 1761 he seems to have provided much, if not all, of the carpentry work (but not the design, as is sometimes claimed) for St. Paul's, the unassuming brick church that still stands — though in considerably altered form — on the east side of Third Street diagonally across from the Powel House. Work on St. Peter's and St. Paul's completed, Smith was free to enter into a contract with the College of Pennsylvania for a new building that until its demolition many years ago stood near the old Whitefield tabernacle on the west side of Fourth Street below Arch. Work for the college continued from 1761 to 1765, and the following year Smith may have been engaged briefly as carpenter on the Alms House, an institution then located in the block bounded on the east and west by Tenth and Eleventh streets and on the north and south by Spruce and Pine. The fact that its occupants needed frequent medical attention made the Alms (or "Bettering") House the forerunner of the Philadelphia General Hospital and provides that institution with the basis for its claim to be the oldest municipal hospital in America.

Probably Smith's association with the Alms House was not extensive or of long duration, for by 1766 we find him employed in the construction of the Third Presbyterian Church, which, as altered to conform to later classical taste, still stands on the south side of Pine Street west of Fourth. The buildings mentioned here were among the most important being erected in Philadelphia at mid-century, and the preeminent position that Smith had by this time achieved among Philadelphia craftsmen is confirmed by his selection by the members of the Carpenters' Company to design their new hall (Fig. 20), noted earlier, which now stands within Independence National Historical Park. In 1769 — a year before Powel — Smith had been elected a member of the American Philosophical Society.

The instructions given Smith by Dr. Kearsley's building committee were so detailed that the design of St. Peter's Church can hardly be said to be his. He is, however, referred to as "architect" — though the eighteenth century gave that title to almost anyone skilled in the erection of buildings — for both the Pine Street Presbyterian Church, mentioned above, and for the new church that the Lutherans began in 1766 on the corner of Cherry and Fourth streets. Though funds were apparently never in hand to complete its impressive steeple, Zion Church was reputedly the largest building of its kind in North America and certainly one of the handsomest. Rebuilt after a disastrous fire in 1794, the church was finally demolished in 1869.

Inevitably, commissions such as this meant also that Smith would come to be known outside his own city. He does not seem to have been "the architect of Philadelphia" who in 1770 expressed an interest in providing the design of a new building for Rhode Island College (now Brown University) in Providence, Rhode Island,[24] as was once thought, but in the same year and doubtless with such buildings as the Alms House and Pennsylvania Hospital in mind, the authorities at Williamsburg did seek his advice concerning a building in which to care for the insane in their city. As begun the following year by the local carpenter Benjamin Powell, the Public Hospital at Williamsburg (burned 1885) is believed to have followed the general lines Smith had suggested.[25]

Presumably the gathering clouds of the Revolution also cast their shadow over Smith's final years. His last public building of importance appears to have been the Walnut Street Prison (demolished 1836), begun in 1773 and considered by some to have been the first penitentiary, though that title belongs not so much to Smith's building as to a smaller one erected to the rear in 1791.[26] Located across from the State House on the southeast corner of Sixth and Walnut streets, where the Penn Mutual building now stands, the Walnut Street Prison may not have been entirely finished in 1777 when Philadelphia was occupied by the British, who found it useful as a place of confinement for their American prisoners. During the early years of the Revolution, Smith was himself concerned with the defenses of the city, to which he contributed the design for the *chevaux-de-frise* that were intended

to aid the guns of Fort Mifflin in obstructing navigation of the Delaware
River. These seem to have worked well enough, but before the colonial
cause could prevail, Smith died on February 11, 1777, at his house on Second
Street, after what *The Pennsylvania Evening Post* described as "a tedious and
painful illness."

Aside from his work for Samuel Powel, we know comparatively little
about Smith's domestic work, which must have been extensive. A contract
(June 4, 1771) to build four two-story houses of brick on property Christ
Church owned on the north side of Spruce between Fourth and Fifth streets
has come to light, as had another dated January 1, 1763, to build two three-
story houses for the Widow Maddox on her lot on Third Street. But Smith's
most famous client was of course Benjamin Franklin, for whom in 1764 he
began a substantial house in a small court off the south side of Market Street
west of Third,[27] and further investigation will almost certainly prove that he
was the builder of numerous Philadelphia houses, including perhaps some of
the large country seats outside the limits of the old city.

In addition to that of Smith, Powel's ledger contains the names of other
craftsmen employed in the alterations to his new dwelling,[28] but in most
cases we can only speculate with varying degrees of probability on the specific
work done by each. Next to Smith, the largest payment went to Hercules
Courtenay, to whom between August 2 and October 5, 1770, Powel paid a
total of £60 "for carving in [his] dwelling House." If he did not already
know of Courtenay, Powel might have become aware of him through advertisements like the one the carver ran in *The Pennsylvania Chronicle* for
August 14–21, 1769, two weeks after the house on Third Street changed
hands:

> Hercules Courtenay, Carver and Gilder, from London, Informs his
> Friends and the Public, that he undertakes all Manner of Carving
> and Gilding, in the newest Taste, at his House in Front-Street, be-
> tween Chestnut and Walnut Streets. N.B. He is determined to be as
> reasonable as possible in his Charges, and to execute all Commands
> with the utmost Diligence.

Cadwalader also paid Courtenay more than £80 to execute the principal
carving for his two parlors, and at a time when Smith was prepared to build
a small brick house for £200, the substantial sum paid by Powel to Courtenay
would indicate work of some importance. But even this did not satisfy the
new owners, who also engaged several other prominent Philadelphia craftsmen to provide additional embellishments. Scarcely a month after making
settlement, Powel paid Nicholas Bernard and Martin Jugiez £7 4s. "for

20. Carpenters' Hall, Independence National Historical Park. Its plan in the form of a Greek cross helped set apart from most eighteenth-century public buildings the hall that Robert Smith designed in 1770 as a headquarters for the Carpenters' Company of the City and County of Philadelphia. Company member Thomas Nevell (1721–1797), who earlier had been in charge of the renovations the John Cadwaladers had made in their house, was engaged to do the joinery on the second floor, which was then leased to the Library Company. Lack of funds probably prevented the carpenters from embellishing the roof of their new hall with the urns its designer intended, and the Revolution was over before the classical decoration of the doorway was put in place. During 1774 the First Continental Congress met here for seven weeks.

carving," and the following June, the noted carver and gilder James Reynolds received £21 6s. more for "sundry carving."

To provide still other decorations, the Powels relied on Timothy Berrett, to whom on November 3 they paid £22 8s. 11d. "for painting & bordering" a room. By "bordering" is presumably meant the application below the cornice of decorative motifs in papier mâché, a material much favored during the Middle Georgian period for its economy and ease of application. Several of Cadwalader's rooms were ornamented in this fashion, though he does not seem to have employed Berrett to do the work. Later, for painting his house, however, Cadwalader did engage Berrett, who apparently specialized in gilding and decorating of a fancy or special nature; at least in 1771 the Pembertons employed him to gild a "wagon" and to ornament it (and possibly other carriages) with a total of four cyphers and four crests.[29] In 1781 Powel also paid Berrett "for extraordinary work on a Phaeton."

Other workmen were employed by Powel for more mundane tasks: during 1769 and 1770 Eden Haydock made charges totaling £16 17s. 4d. for painter's and plumber's work; on October 19 Jacob Graff was paid £3 4s. for "putting in windows"; about the same time Thomas Paschall was paid £4 12s. 7d. "for sundry ironmongery," and over the next few months Benjamin Armitage received a total of £18 9s. 1d. for work of a similar nature. At present there seems no way of knowing precisely to what charges of this kind refer; the £15 5s. 4d. paid Casper Geier on December 17 "for marble work," on the other hand, may well refer to the Pennsylvania marble that must have surrounded the principal fireplaces. Not only are the front steps not of marble, but this feature, which Geier had charged Cadwalader £10 14s. 1d. to provide, would presumably already have been in place when Powel bought the house from Stedman. It was several months before the new owners got around to improving the cellar, but in July of 1770 John Palmer was paid £14 19s. 5d. for arching and paving that portion of the house, where Patrick Waaugh also dug a well.[30]

With servants at work or quartered in the garret and back buildings, there was need for some device to summon them to the door or to the main rooms of the house. For this purpose Thomas Hale "Carpenter, from London," advertised that he was prepared to undertake "the Business of hanging Bells (through all the Apartments of Houses, Ships, Stores etc.) in the most neat and lasting Manner."[31] One of the first things the Powels did after purchasing their new house was to engage Hale's services, and additional payments were made to him later the same year. Hale's principal competitor in Philadelphia seems to have been Alexander Smith, who supplied bells for the Cadwaladers, and Powel's accounts also record substantial payments to

Smith during 1769 "for Smith's Works." In 1771 Powel paid Smith an additional £12.

Despite the many fine houses in eighteenth-century Philadelphia, advertisements run by the workmen employed by Powel suggest that there was not enough construction in progress at one time to provide steady employment for the master craftsmen living in the city, many of whom were obliged to supplement income from their trade or craft with earnings from other sources. In Baltimore, Courtenay had operated a general store and after coming to Philadelphia sold candles and soap;[32] at their looking-glass shop on the corner of Third and Chestnut streets, Bernard & Jugiez offered for sale "curious and ornamental prints" as well as "figures of plaister of Paris";[33] and even Reynolds, whose carving is so much esteemed by modern collectors, advertised as available at his store on Front Street such items as glue, painting materials, leaf gold, umbrellas, paper hangings, and papier mâché brackets and ornaments for ceilings.[34]

Plan

In the course of his sojourn in Philadelphia the Marquis de Chastellux observed that the handsome dwelling of Robert Morris on Market Street "closely resemble[d] the houses in London."[35] With this judgment of the principal source for the design of the Georgian houses of Philadelphia — especially those like Powel's or Morris's that belong to the most highly developed type — modern historians have generally agreed, though war and the changing patterns of urban life have left few examples for comparison in either city.[36]

Of course most Philadelphians occupied comparatively simple quarters — often with only one room on each level[37] — but the first-floor plan of Powel's dwelling was one that experience had proved efficient and practical for larger city houses (Fig. 21). At one side, the passage was made to serve several functions: it led to the service wing at the back, it afforded ready and separate access to the two principal rooms on the ground floor; and when slightly widened at the rear, it provided space from which the stair might conveniently rise to one or more levels above.

When they gave them any name at all, many eighteenth-century Philadelphians continued to refer to the principal rooms on the ground floor of their city houses as "parlors," and those between the first level and the garret as "chambers." Since by no means all chambers contained sleeping accommodations, they cannot be equated with the modern bedroom, however. The word "hall," which had designated the most essential room in the late medieval house — and by extension the whole structure, as in the case of

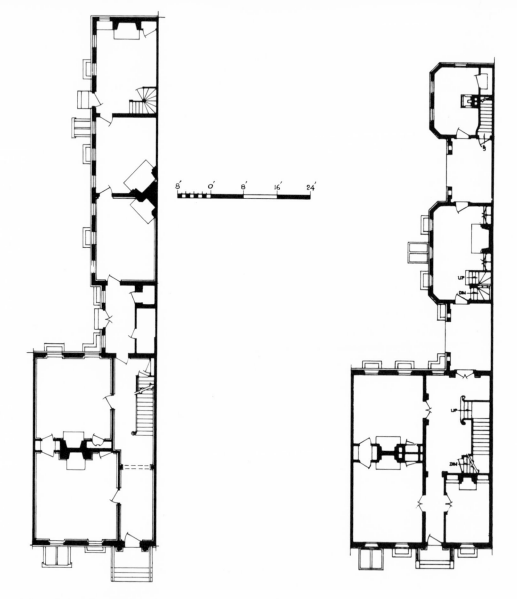

21. *Left.* Plan of the ground floor of the Powel House. Drawn in 1975 by Lancelot F. Sims, Jr., A. I. A. Though conjectural in some details, the plan reproduced here probably reflects fairly closely the form the house had assumed by 1785.

22. *Right.* Conjectural plan of a four-bay house. Based in part on a drawing sometimes attributed to Samuel Rhoads and published by Wainwright; redrawn in 1975, by Lancelot F. Sims, Jr., A. I. A. The Willing house a few yards to the north of the Powels' was apparently of this general type, but it was demolished long ago, as were all the Philadelphia houses that had a door and three windows on the facade. In common with other plans illustrated here, the arrangement of rooms in a four-bay house was capable of a mirror reversal, and of course the stairs might be either behind the small adjacent room (as here and in the Cadwalader house) or in front of it (as in the Masters-Penn-Morris house). In their details the back buildings must also have varied considerably.

"Haddon Hall" or "Kirby Hall" — had generally passed out of use as referring to a room, without as yet fully assuming its modern meaning of an intermediate space used to promote ease of circulation, a feature that in Philadelphia during the Early and Middle Georgian periods was usually called simply the "passage." As they had earlier, most rooms continued to be thought of as serving a variety of purposes, and only rarely is any specific function indicated by the use of such a prefix as "dining."

Though the plan of the Powel House conformed in general character to that widely used in the mid-eighteenth century for Philadelphia houses of the better sort, a number of variations were possible. For example, a corner lot permitted a door on the side, with consequent shortening of the entrance passage and in its place the introduction of a small front room, as in the case of the Shippen-Wistar house (Figs. 23 and 24). When the lot was sufficiently wide, the entrance of the house might be placed in the center of the facade with a front room of equal size on either side, thereby creating a five-bay or "double house."[38] The old Shippen mansion, mentioned earlier, had a symmetrical, five-bay facade, and a later example may still be seen in the Reynolds-Morris house on South Eighth Street (Figs. 25 and 26).

Lying somewhere between the three-bay plan of the Powel House and the five-bay, "double" house were others like that of the Cadwaladers where a width of about forty feet permitted on one side of the passage a full-sized parlor and on the other a small room, with space for the stair either in front or behind (Fig. 22). This was essentially the plan that Isaac Ware regarded as typical of London in the mid-eighteenth century:

> The common houses . . . are all built in one way [he wrote], and that so familiar that it will need little instruction. The general custom is to make two rooms and a light closet on a floor. . . . The first floor [i.e. that at the second level] in these common houses consists of the dining room, over the hall or parlour; a bed-chamber over the back parlour, and a closet over its closet.[39]

Probably four-bay houses of this kind occupied a more important place in the history of Philadelphia architecture than has been generally supposed. The Masters-Penn-Morris house, which served as the presidential residence in Philadelphia for both Washington and Adams, is now recognized as having been of this type,[40] as was apparently that of Franklin. At least, in a survey made August 5, 1766, by the Philadelphia Contributionship, the latter is described as having "3 rooms on a floor."[41]

To the rear of the main house were regularly the "back buildings" in which were housed one or more kitchens and such other service functions as

23. Shippen-Wistar house, Fourth and Locust (Prune) Streets. Probably built about 1767–68 for Dr. William Shippen, Jr., and his wife Alice Lee of Stratford, Virginia; occupied from 1798 to 1818 by Dr. Caspar Wistar, who, like Shippen, was professor of anatomy at the University of Pennsylvania. Despite the prominence of its early occupants, this Middle Georgian dwelling belongs in the category of important houses that were never intended by their owners to approach the grandeur of those belonging to other Philadelphians like the Powels or the Cadwaladers. The doorway on the north facade, shown here, has been restored to conform to descriptions in insurance surveys made in the nineteenth century. The Late Georgian house to the south was built about 1828 for Joseph Parker Norris and was purchased in 1837 by Judge John Cadwalader. Today both the Norris-Cadwalader and the Shippen-Wistar houses have been admirably adapted for use as headquarters by the Mutual Assurance Company.

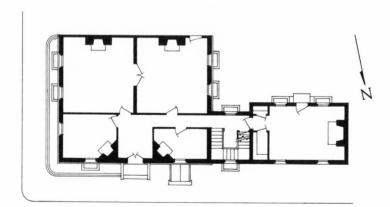

24. Plan of the ground floor of the Shippen-Wistar house. Based in part on the Old Philadelphia Survey and redrawn in 1975 by Lancelot F. Sims, Jr., A. I. A. Though corner houses such as this must once have been numerous in Georgian Philadelphia, few remain and no others of the quality of this one. As shown here, the original stairs appear to have been located in the passage that connected the main house with its back building, now demolished.

25. Reynolds-Morris house, 225 South Eighth Street. Erected in 1786–87 for William Reynolds, a "Doctor of Physick," this is today the best surviving example of the five-bay or "double" house occasionally built in Philadelphia during the Georgian period. The simple interior conforms closely to the first description of the house now known, an insurance survey of 1830. On the exterior, a date after the Revolution is indicated by flatter surfaces and more slender proportions, but in most other respects there is little to distinguish this design from that of houses built earlier in the century. Privately owned.

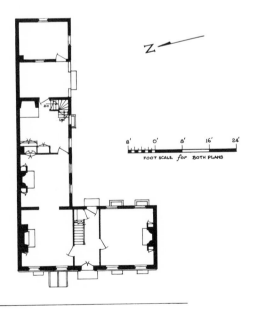

26. Plan of the ground floor of the Reynolds-Morris house. Based on the Old Philadelphia Survey and redrawn in 1975 by Lancelot F. Sims, Jr., A. I. A. As was the case earlier, the rooms of houses such as this must have continued to serve a variety of purposes. That at the right of the stair hall was probably the principal parlor; that on the left may have been a second or dining parlor, with a "sitting room," possibly used by the family or as a servants' hall, behind it. Behind this was the kitchen with its larger fireplace for cooking, and beyond that, across an open piazza, was the wash house.

the laundry. Even when these utilitarian structures were of the same height and joined together to form a single unit, as in the case of the Powel House, it was often customary to speak of them in the plural, as did Stedman in the advertisements by which he sought to sell his house on Third Street. Contrary to what was once thought, cellar kitchens were also used occasionally in the eighteenth century.[42] Probably the location of his house in the restricted area of a court obliged Franklin to adopt this form in place of the more usual line of back buildings, and presumably decreasing space for building also helps to explain why cellar kitchens were more popular with nineteenth-century Philadelphians than with their colonial predecessors.

Because they were of different heights, three back buildings are described separately in the survey of the Byrd-Penn-Chew house (Appendix III), which stood next to the Powels', but these structures may well have been contiguous or nearly so. Certainly by the middle of the eighteenth century, considerations of space and convenience were leading Philadelphians to prefer back buildings situated near the main house and linked to it by an enclosed passage or at least by some kind of covered walkway as protection from the weather. Especially when open on the sides, such connecting members were sometimes called "piazzas" in the eighteenth century, and the back buildings they joined to the main house may conveniently be spoken of as being "semidetached" to distinguish them from completely separate structures or from those connected by an enclosed passage like that at the Powel House. *Piazza* is an Italian word that refers to a square or open space, and its use in this case recalls such European squares as London's Covent Garden, which were at least partly surrounded by covered walkways that protected pedestrians from the weather in much the same way as did the connecting links of colonial buildings. The use of *piazza* in this context is not only an interesting example of how the name of the whole may be transferred to one of its parts,[43] but also a reminder of which country it was that originated the Renaissance vocabulary made familiar to American craftsmen and their clients through the use of English architectural books and builder's guides. Structural evidence suggests that the present brick passage that links the Powel House with its back building was not built at the same time as the main house — and therefore may not have been planned from the first — though there seems no good reason to suppose that it was not there during the Powels' occupancy.

Rooms on the second and third levels of Philadelphia houses repeated in most essentials the plan of those on the first. An exception was the front chamber at the second level, which in the absence of any need for a passage giving access to the street, might on occasion be permitted to extend the full width of the house. As further embellished by the Powels, this front chamber became easily the most notable part of their city residence.

Lit adequately by dormer windows, two or more rooms in the garret provided additional space for children or for household servants.

Facade

From his familiar reference to "a greene Country Towne, which will never be burnt, and allwayes be wholsome," it may be inferred that Penn visualized the future houses of Philadelphia as standing in the midst of their orchards and gardens. Some of the first dwellings did conform to this pattern, and even in Powel's day a few of the newer houses, like that of the Cadwaladers,[44] stood well back from the street. But even from the earliest days of the city, poor roads and English precedent had led most Philadelphians to prefer contiguous houses with a garden in the rear but no yard in front. The Stedmans and the Byrds were therefore only conforming to fashionable London practice when they built their houses in this manner. And since balance was a guiding principle of Renaissance design, builders of three-bay and four-bay Georgian houses doubtless expected the asymmetry that inevitably resulted from having to place their front doors off-center would be obviated to some degree when one facade was seen in relation to others on either side. Presumably it was considerations of this kind that underlay Stedman's decision to make the width and height of his new house similar to that of the Governor with which it shared a party wall on the north.

From this it should not be inferred that the two houses were identical, however. A survey made of the Byrd-Penn-Chew house in 1770 by the same Gunning Bedford who had described Powel's house the year before shows, in fact, a number of interesting differences (Appendix III). For one, the doorway (usually referred to in the eighteenth century as the "frontispiece") of the governor's house was framed by the Ionic order, though the Roman Doric columns selected by Stedman were probably more typical of the bold doorways that about 1750 emerge as one of the most readily identifiable features of the Middle Georgian style. It was in that year, or the next, that Edmund Woolley used just such a doorway on the exterior of the tower he added to the south side of the State House (Fig. 27).

Though certainly not without precedent, the omission of a pitched pediment on the State House doorway was somewhat unusual and may have been forced on Woolley by the nearness of the Palladian window above. But whatever its sources, in the wake of its use on the State House, this type of frontispiece became a distinguishing characteristic of a number of Philadelphia buildings,[45] including the Powel House, though the traditional triangular pediment was probably more popular. The latter was selected for illustration in its *Articles and Rules* by the Carpenters' Company, and variants may still be seen among extant examples outside the city at Mount Pleasant (Fig. 13) and Woodford in Fairmount Park, as well as at Cliveden (Fig. 14) in Germantown — all noted earlier as the country houses that best illustrate the Middle Georgian style in the Philadelphia area.

For a pedimented doorway from another city mansion contemporary with the Powel House, we are fortunate in having the frontispiece re-erected in the Philadelphia Museum of Art after the house once occupied by the Reverend Robert Blackwell was demolished earlier in the twentieth century (Fig. 28).[46] Blackwell's doorway does share with Powel's, however, the eight panels in the jamb that echo so effectively those of the door, a feature that follows closely the example illustrated by the Carpenters' Company and therefore one that must have been common in Philadelphia.

As befits its later date and domestic purpose, the doorway of Powel's house (Fig. 29) is lighter and more graceful in its proportions than that used earlier by Woolley at the State House, an effect that results in part from the substitution of Ionic dentils (small, square blocks) for the usual Doric entablature with its heavier triglyphs, metopes, and mutules. Sanctioned by Roman practice, variations and combinations of this kind had been approved by numerous Renaissance architects, though the specific form taken in this case may well have been influenced by the Ionic frontispiece of the Governor's house next door.

We have at present no way of knowing the names of any of the craftsmen engaged by Stedman, but quite possibly the columns for his doorway were supplied by John Elmslie, who seems to have made a practice of turning them from cedar for £2 a pair. Then as now, craftsmen working in the "best manner" would cover the top of a flat entablature with a piece of lead to prevent damage from the weather, a precaution that in this case doubtless helps to account for the good condition in which Powel's doorway has survived the passage of two centuries. If Stedman included the customary brass knocker with his house, either something happened to it or it was not to Powel's taste, for on April 1, 1773, he paid the brass founder Daniel King £1 for a new one. Presumably this was the type of knocker that King advertised as being his own invention and "peculiarly singular" in that it was proof against being "wrenched from off" its owner's door "through the wanton frolicks of sundry intoxicated bucks and blades."[47]

As was regularly the case with even the best Georgian buildings in the colonies, both materials and workmanship employed for the brick facade of the Powel House were superior to those found on the exposed side and at the

27. *Left.* South doorway to the tower of the State House (Independence Hall). Added about 1753 by Edmund Woolley (d. 1771), the carpenter-architect who had also been in charge of erecting the earlier portion of the building. As first constructed between 1732 and 1748, the State House had no tower, and access to the upper story was from the central passage. The tower was begun about 1750 in a manner that might be said to usher in the Middle Georgian style in Philadelphia, though the doorway without pediment was a form favored by Abraham Swan, the English designer whose books were popular with Philadelphia craftsmen.

28. *Right.* Front doorway from the Blackwell house. Originally erected at 224 Pine Street and traditionally dated 1764; removed to the Philadelphia Museum of Art about 1925. To prevent the frontispiece from assuming an ungainly height, the semicircular transom required to light the passage might be permitted to extend into the triangular space (tympanum) of the pediment, as here. When this was done, classic canons required that a piece of the entablature (Doric triglyphs and mutules in this case) had to be kept above each column. A fanlight with Gothic sash, precisely like that in the Blackwell house doorway, appeared as Plate XII in the *Articles and Rules* of the Carpenters' Company and was there listed among the more expensive types available. But cost was not likely to be an obstacle for the Reverend Robert Blackwell, who was not only assistant to Doctor (later Bishop) William White and the rector of nearby St. Peter's Church but also one of the richest men in the city. Courtesy, Philadelphia Museum of Art, The Temple Fund, 1921.

rear. Laws against dumping ballast in the harbors and the poor condition of most colonial roads sometimes made it economical to use brick imported from England or Holland, but in view of the number and quality of Philadelphia's own brick yards, there seems no good reason to look elsewhere for the source of the superior bricks laid here in Flemish bond (i.e. alternating "headers" and "stretchers" in the same course). Smoother and more uniform, the "face" bricks of the best Philadelphia houses were often slightly larger than the "common" bricks employed elsewhere in the building. The larger size of the face bricks was, in turn, accompanied by the use of narrower mortar joints, which were first cut flush and then marked with a straight line, a process known as "rodding" and widely used by colonial masons for many kinds of brickwork.[48]

The emphasis placed on the facades of Georgian buildings is a reflection of the general concern with elegance of effect characteristic of Renaissance architecture and is not indicative of the builder's carelessness with detail or of the parsimony of his client. Because it took longer to lay and was therefore more expensive than other brick patterns in common use, Flemish bond was frequently limited to the facades of Georgian buildings. Only for such fine houses as Stedman's would it be used on the rear as well as on the front. Viewed in this context, it is significant that the south side of the Powel House is now laid in cheaper common bond (all stretchers with only an occasional row of headers). If this accurately reflects the original brickwork, it can only mean that Stedman expected that in due course another house would be erected on the adjacent lot, thereby obscuring the south wall he was building.

Above the windows of the Powel House are to be seen the usual flat arches of gauged (dressed to size) brick with decorative keystones of "granite."[49] The latter material was also used for the two belt courses that define the three levels of the Powel House and thereby provide the kind of strong horizontal accents that help to give Georgian buildings their distinctive char-

29. *Opposite*. Lower portion of the facade of the Powel House. Had he desired Ionic capitals, Stedman would have had to employ a carver as well as a carpenter and a turner to ornament the doorway of his new house, and this may help to explain why a frontispiece in the Doric order was the only kind illustrated in the *Articles and Rules* of the Carpenters' Company and the type most favored in Georgian Philadelphia.

acter. Conclusive evidence for the color of the paint originally used on the exterior of the Powel House has not come to light, but since in their search for elegance eighteenth-century builders had no prejudice against treating an inferior material to resemble a more imposing one, probably most of the exposed wood on the exterior of colonial buildings was originally painted to suggest the stone used on their English prototypes and perhaps elsewhere on the same structure for belt courses, keystones, and the like. Indeed, the effective contrast of light trim against red brick walls early became — and long remained — characteristic of Philadelphia, a city that received its initial inspiration from the London that emerged after the Great Fire of 1666.

In essence, all of the foregoing features were duplicated in varying scale and quality on the facades of hundreds of Philadelphia houses in the eighteenth century. Customary also was the sloping wooden door or bulkhead that provided an outside entrance from the sidewalk to the cellar. On country houses exterior shutters are not thought to have been common much before the middle of the century, but in cities the greater need for security may have prompted their use at an earlier date. Toward the end of the eighteenth century the familiar type of louvered shutter was widely favored for windows above the ground floor, but the panel variety used at all levels of the Powel House are mentioned in the survey of 1859 and were found on the house when purchased by the Landmarks Society. The simple wrought-iron railings that flank the front steps also have a long history, though exactly when they were set up has not been determined.

By 1930 the original modillioned eaves described in Bedford's survey of 1769 had disappeared.[50] The present ones are therefore necessary replacements, as are all the window sash, now 12 over 12 on the first two stories and 8 over 8 in the smaller windows on the third.[51] Time and men have dealt more kindly with the dormers, which are of the "arched or niche" type with "plain scrowl [scroll] brackets" (best seen in Figure 40), one of the four standard designs illustrated in the *Articles and Rules* of the Carpenters' Company. The same source pictures "Gothic" sash as an alternate window treatment, though their repetition here in the transom above the front door was perhaps uncommon. Today the dormers of the Powel House appear much as they did when the house was purchased by the Landmarks Society and are presumably a part of the original fabric, especially since its inaccessibility made this feature traditionally among the last to be altered or destroyed, as a glance along almost any of the older streets of Philadelphia will serve to confirm.

Other exterior features of the Powel House have not fared so well. Long gone are the "electrical Rods" invented and popularized by Dr. Franklin, for which John Bissell was paid £6 3s. 9d., while the original "lead spouts," which helped protect walls and trim from the weather, had an even briefer history. They were sacrificed to the needs of the colonial army in August of 1777, though Powel later received £44 19s. in compensation.[52]

It is tempting to see the severe exteriors of even the most important Philadelphia houses as a reflection of the Quaker origins of the city and the emphasis that sect placed upon the virtues of sobriety and moderation. Such influences are not to be overlooked, of course, but it should be noted that these same qualities are also found in English buildings erected during the early years of the Hanoverian dynasty when the most restrained facades often hid interiors that today appear opulent to the point of vulgarity. Probably the exterior of the Powel House is therefore less a reflection of Quaker esthetic than of the supposed Roman virtue of *gravitas*,[53] so much admired by Whig owners and designers in England. If this interpretation is correct, it helps to confirm the belief that during the eighteenth century Philadelphia conformed more closely to current English practice than did most other American cities.

Passage and Stair

The most important part of the original fabric of the Powel House to remain in place on the interior is the fine mahogany stair and the lower passage from which it rises (Fig. 30). Lit principally by the transom over the front door, the generous proportions and handsome detailing of the entrance passage provide a suitable introduction to the grandeur that lies beyond.

After the house had been acquired by the Landmarks Society, the woodwork of the passage was returned by the Philadelphia Museum of Art, which had earlier removed it to prevent its loss. As reinstalled, the passage today looks much as it did in old photographs taken for postcards early in the twentieth century (Fig. 31), when this was one of the few portions of the house sufficiently intact to serve that purpose. Here are still to be seen wainscoting to the height of the chair-rail ("pedestal high"), the pediments over the doors, and the "dentil cornish" (cornice) mentioned in the 1769 survey and therefore part of the original embellishments installed by Stedman. Mentioned also in the 1769 survey are the handsomely "fluted pilasters" that support an arch marking a point at which the passage widens slightly to accommodate the stairs that rise along the north wall. These (and perhaps other features added by Powel, but now lost) impressed the author of the 1785 survey as deserving the words "highly ornamented" — a descriptive phrase he reserved for this area and the large front chamber above. Clearly, the Stedmans and Powels intended that the first impression on entering their house should be one of opulence.

30. *Opposite*. Entrance passage of the Powel House. Though this is one of the few examples to survive, entrance passages must often have been among the most lavishly decorated features of important Middle Georgian houses in Philadelphia. In addition to cornices of various kinds, the passage of Alexander Stedman's house had "Double pilasters of the Corinthian Order," and that at the Masters-Penn-Morris house had two fluted columns, four pilasters, and four arches.

31. *Above*. Entrance passage of the Powel House in 1908. Franklin D. Edmunds made this photograph for the postcard series he marketed under the name "Old Colonial." Today it helps confirm the authenticity of the entrance passage as now constituted and incidentally of the back building, part of which may be glimpsed through the doorway in the rear.

32. Landing of the front stair of the Powel House. Only the finest Middle Georgian houses had mahogany stairs that, as here, made an open turn about fluted newel posts and were furnished with mahogany wainscot to match.

Broad enough for even the most amply gowned figure, the stair installed by Stedman was of the finest type available in eighteenth-century Philadelphia. In the terminology of the day, these are "open newel stairs"; in contrast to the tight "winders" found in smaller houses or in the back buildings of great ones, here wide treads rise by easy stages to make a complete turn around a pair of fluted newel posts (Fig. 32).[54] Balusters were usually sup-

33. Powel House stair, detail of twist. Fine as it was, the Powels' stair was not the most elaborate that Philadelphia craftsmen were prepared to supply. Instead of the single twist seen here, John Dickinson's stair terminated in a twist of two revolutions. Though the newel appears in good condition in Edmund's photograph (Fig. 31), it was later damaged and had to be restored when the Landmarks Society acquired the house.

plied by "turners," rather than by carpenters, and are found in an almost infinite number of variations; examples similar — but not identical — to those in the Powel House are illustrated in many of the English architectural books. At each newel the sweep of the hand rail is broken by a short upward curve topped by a horizontal straight section, while at the lower end the rail terminates in a single "twist" (Fig. 33). And this pattern of newel and "ramped" rail is reflected in lower profile on the wall beside the stair, where is also repeated the "pedestal-high" wainscot carried throughout the first story. Like the bolder frontispieces, noted earlier, stairs of this character are among the most notable features of the Middle Georgian style, the handsome twist, in particular, standing in marked contrast to the simple squared post of late Jacobean character that may still be seen in such Early Georgian houses as Stenton or Bellaire (Fig. 34).

As in the case of other stairs of this quality, Stedman's were "bracketed"; that is, decorated on the open side by ornamental brackets in the triangular space formed by the treads and risers. The present plain brackets are modern replacements that reflect the general shape of the lost originals, the profiles of which could still be seen in the paint when the house was acquired by the Landmarks Society. So fine a stair might be expected to have carved brackets like those provided by Samuel Harding for the State House (Fig. 35), however, and possibly we should see here a task assigned to one of the expert carvers Powel employed shortly after purchasing the house. If we assume that the insurance surveys are accurate in such details (Appendix I), it seems clear that at least Powel did alter the stairway to the extent of replacing pine with mahogany at the second level. Only stairs in prominent positions in the finest houses were usually of mahogany; Cadwalader, for example, contented himself with painted pine, presumably because his stairway was placed to one side, behind the small front parlor, and therefore out of view of the front door.[55] Like other rooms on the ground level, the passage of the Powel House retains its original floor composed of wide (4½ to 6 inches) boards of yellow pine held together by horizontal dowels and plastered on the under-side in the belief that this would increase resistance to fire. The best (and most expensive) then available, doweled floors of this kind were desired because they were tighter and less likely to warp. The lock with which Powel secured his front door had been removed by the time the house was acquired by the Landmarks Society, but the present one of cast iron with brass fittings is said to be the original, which was returned and repaired in 1936.

Preliminary research shows the original paint in the passage to have been a light green, followed by a pinkish beige.[56]

The upper passage, to which the stairs lead, has been restored to conform to that on the ground floor.[57]

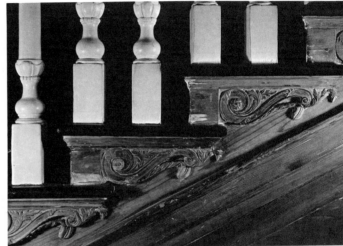

34. *Left*. Stairway of Bellaire. Built about 1720 south of the old city proper in what is now called Franklin D. Roosevelt Park. The handsome turnings characteristic of much seventeenth-century and early eighteenth-century work did not extend to the newel posts, which were generally severely rectangular, as here. Boldly paneled wainscot also covered many of the interior walls of important Early Georgian houses. For its time and place that in the parlor at Bellaire is unsurpassed in quality. Now owned by the City of Philadelphia.

35. *Right*. Brackets from the stairway of the State House (Independence Hall). Carved by Samuel Harding about 1753. Models for ornamental stair brackets could easily be found in the English design books of Abraham Swan and others. Originally the stair of the Powel House may have shared this feature with other major examples of Middle Georgian architecture, both in Philadelphia and elsewhere in the American colonies. In *Colonial Grandeur in Philadelphia* Wainwright tells of twenty-three such brackets that in 1772 Hercules Courtenay carved for John Dickinson at a cost of 4s. 6d. each. No longer fashionable, these were discarded when the Dickinson house was demolished in 1826 to make way for John Haviland's Philadelphia Arcade on Chestnut Street west of Sixth. Photograph by Jack Boucher for the Historic American Buildings Survey.

Front Room Downstairs

To judge from contemporary descriptions, the front room on the ground floor seems to have been the parlor in most Philadelphia residences of the Middle-Georgian period and hence the most important part of the house in terms of its decoration. That of Alexander Stedman, for example, was his only room "wainscoted up to the ceiling"; similarly, that in the Byrd-Penn-Chew house next door to Powel's was "wainscoted all through" and ornamented with a "fret cornish" (Appendix III), while we know that Cadwalader lavished many of his richest improvements on this portion of his house.

Despite the well-defined Philadelphia practice of using the front room on the ground floor as the principal parlor, there seems to have been nothing especially remarkable about this part of the Powels' house. The survey of 1769 mentions briefly two rooms on the first floor, both of which were wainscoted only to the chair-rail ("pedestal high"), and there is no indication in the survey of 1785 that any significant changes had been made during the fifteen-year interval since the first policy had been taken out. Probably it was no coincidence that in his surveys Gunning Bedford lists a front "room" in Powel's house but a front "parlor" in that of both Governor Penn and John Cadwalader.

When an adjoining house was built on the Powels' old garden about 1825, it necessarily eliminated all the windows in what now became a party wall. In the downstairs front room the two windows originally on the south wall have therefore had to be replaced. Restored also are all the window sash, the broken pediment over the door leading into the front passage, and both the mantel and overmantel. The model used in restoring the latter two features was provided by the back room upstairs, now in the Metropolitan Museum of Art (Fig. 54), and, except for the entrance passage, the only major portion of the house that has come down to the twentieth century essentially intact. Not only was this the most practical course to follow, but further authority for it is provided by the two eighteenth-century surveys that have proved so useful in other respects: that of 1785 describes the front room as being "finished in [the] same stile" as the one behind it, while both the 1769 and 1785 surveys agree that the back room downstairs, in turn, resembled the one above. With its restored "tabernacle frame" above the mantel, cornice of Ionic dentils, wainscoting below the chair-rail, and "windows cased with architraves round" the front room today corresponds closely to that described in the eighteenth-century surveys (Fig. 36).

36. Front room downstairs in the Powel House. The blind door at the right of the fireplace was a device not infrequently employed by Georgian builders to provide the symmetry that contributed to the sense of formal elegance that was their overriding concern. Similar false doors are made to flank the parlor fireplace at Mount Pleasant in order to balance two opposite doorways that lead from the central passage. The camera lens has made this room appear larger than approximately twenty by twenty feet, its true dimensions.

Several persons who remembered the Powel House as it appeared in the late nineteenth century recalled having seen there a number of "ivory door-knobs," at least one of which is known to have been available to those who removed and restored rooms from the house in the 1920s.[58] The fact that neither they nor those who later restored the house itself used hardware of this kind can only mean that it was regarded as not being part of the original fabric. The brass handles and escutcheons now used in the house are high-quality reproductions, most of which are based on marks left on the old doors and on a single example believed to have come from the house and now re-installed on the blind door at the right of the fireplace in the front room downstairs (Fig. 37).[59] In many of the doors the interior mechanism that works the lock and latch is old and presumably the original.

Here, too, should perhaps be mentioned the common Georgian practice of importing a marble mantel for at least one of the principal rooms of the house. Features of this kind will be recalled in such notable Virginia houses as Westover, Gunston Hall, and Mount Vernon, and there is evidence that Powel also imported such a mantel. At least we know from his ledger that on August 18, 1770 — or just a year after purchasing Stedman's house — he paid 17s. 6d. to Gideon Villeneuf "for freight of a chimney-piece." Of course to the extent that they reflected current English taste, imports of this kind inevitably looked somewhat out of place in their more backward colonial surroundings, a situation that has probably led to the removal of more than one such mantel by over-zealous modern "restorers."[60] Under these circumstances the fact that a marble mantel was removed from the front room when the Powel House was restored might be cause for concern were it not that the two "Clouded marble mantels," mentioned in the survey of 1859 (Appendix II), do indeed have a nineteenth-century ring.

If an inventory of his household furnishings was made at the time of Powel's death, it has not come to light, but even if one were to be found, it would probably tell us little about the specific purposes served by rooms of this kind. Was it here, perhaps, that General Washington was received on those occasions when he came for tea? Partly with this possibility in mind, the front room of the Powel House has been furnished with a typical Philadelphia table of the period set for tea. The oblong tables common in New England were certainly made by craftsmen like Benjamin Randolph, but the more usual Philadelphia form was round, its tilting top hinged on a "bird-cage" support. This device made it easy to store such tables against the wall or in a corner, from which they could be brought out whenever needed.

37. Brass drop-handles and pierced escutcheon. Believed to have been part of the original hardware of the Powel House and the model for the reproductions used in its restoration. Details of this kind would ordinarily have been ordered from England, often from catalogs that were available for the purpose. Photograph by Berry & Homer, about 1933.

Back Room Downstairs

Both the survey of 1769 and that of 1785 identify the second room on the ground floor of the Powel House (Fig. 38) as simply the "back room," but the presence there of a buffet (cupboard) for the storage and display of china and silver has suggested that this was probably where the owners customarily took their meals.

The practice of designating a particular place for eating is at least as old as Roman times, but more direct sources for the modern dining room are to be sought in Tudor England, when persons of wealth set aside a special room in which they might dine with some degree of privacy. By the early eighteenth century, "dyning parlors" or "dineing roomes" begin to be mentioned occasionally in colonial inventories, though the commonplace character of the furnishing listed suggests that in many cases such rooms were probably used by family and possibly by household servants, while guests were still served in the best parlor or perhaps even in the entrance hall, when that area of the house retained a part of its earlier character and importance, as at Stenton. In an era when slaves and other household servants were plentiful, convenience, in the modern sense, did not count for much, and there was nothing to prevent formal dining upstairs in one of the chambers, especially when that was the most handsomely decorated part of the house, as is the case at Mount Pleasant or at the Powel House.

Not until the end of the eighteenth century — and therefore essentially after the period here under discussion — did such specialized furnishings as the extension table and sideboard equipped with drawers and cupboards become easily available in the colonies. The forerunner of the familiar Hepplewhite sideboard was the serving (or side) table,[61] and probably the pre-Revolutionary furnishings of the Powels' back room included at least one of these, possibly equipped with a marble top as a precaution against damage by heat and alcohol. By the third quarter of the eighteenth century the earlier type of round, gate-legged dining table with turned supports and drop leaves had given way to new forms associated with the name of Thomas Chippendale (c. 1718–1779), the popular English cabinetmaker whose *Gentleman & Cabinet-Maker's Director* first appeared in 1754. Though not illustrated in the *Director,* one of the most useful and innovative of these later designs was the "set" of three or more drop-leaf tables that could be joined together in various combinations to accommodate groups of different sizes. When not in use, such tables might be placed out of the way against the wall — possibly even in the passage — and then easily carried to any of the principal rooms in the house when it came time to set them up for dining. The large front chamber on the second level of the Powels' house would have lent itself admirably to the use of a large set of tables of this kind. It was probably there, rather than in this smaller room, that the Powels entertained in a manner lavish enough to shock a New England conscience. Under the date of September 8, 1774, John Adams noted in his diary:

> Dined at Mr. Powells, with Mr. Duché, Dr. Morgan, Dr. Steptoe, Mr. Goldsborough, Mr. Johnson, and many others. — A most sinfull Feast again! Every Thing which could delight the Eye, or allure the Taste, Curds and Creams, Jellies, Sweet meats of various sorts, 20 sorts of Tarts, fools, Trifles, floating Islands, whipped Sillabubs &c. &c. — Parmesan Cheese, Punch, Wine, Porter, Beer.[62]

If only Adams had thought to tell us in what part of his host's house he had dined so sumptuously.

38. Back room downstairs in the Powel House. Like other pediments throughout the house, that over the door leading to the main passage had to be restored, as did also the windows in the west wall. With its ornament of Ionic dentils, simple cornices like this one were widely used in the better Philadelphia houses of the period. Next door, the Byrd-Penn-Chew house had several rooms decorated in this fashion, and Alexander Stedman's house had such a "Dentile Cornish" throughout. Again, the camera has enhanced the apparent size of the room.

39. Chimney breast, back room downstairs, before restoration. Though details of the mantel and overmantel are necessarily conjectural, the location of the pediment and shelf was clearly indicated by traces of the originals visible on the surviving paneling of the chimney breast. The upper corners of the door frames that flank the fireplace are broken out in characteristic "knees," each of which retains in the center the small square of carving that Powel's workmen would probably have referred to as a "flower." Photograph by Berry & Homer, Philadelphia, 1937.

By the time the Powel House was restored, the mantel and overmantel of the back room had been removed, probably by Isaiah Hacker, who would have replaced it with the "clouded marble" one mentioned in the survey of 1859. The paneling of the chimney breast (Fig. 39) survives, however, and the present restoration is based on evidence provided by this and by the mantel and overmantel of the room above, which survives intact in the Metropolitan Museum of Art (Fig. 54) and which the surveys of 1769 and 1785 describe as being similar to that of the room below. Probably the original differed principally from the one we see today in being somewhat plainer: the pineapple in the broken pediment is certainly an imaginative touch supplied by the restorer, and the carved details would have been more appropriate to one of the rooms upstairs that were used for entertaining than to one downstairs that may have served as the dining parlor for the family.

Back Buildings

Possibly because it seemed to offer fewer problems and those that could be solved at least cost, the back building was one of the first parts of the Powel House to be restored by the Landmarks Society (Fig. 40). Beyond noting its length and that it was "large, convenient . . . and two stories high," Stedman's advertisement did not describe this part of the house he was offering for sale. From the survey of 1769, however, we learn that there were originally three rooms on each of the two floors and that these were "finished well and painted inside and out."

To this general description, the survey of 1785 contributes the additional fact that at the ground level the low wainscoting characteristic of the front rooms was by then extended beyond the passage into the first room of the back building, thereby linking it to the main living area of the house rather than to the service functions beyond. The survey of 1769 does not give this first room a name, but in the survey of 1785 it is called the "nursery," a term that reflects general Philadelphia practice rather than that specifically of the Powels, the last of whose sons had died in infancy ten years before. Since its nearness to the kitchen would have made this one of the warmest rooms in the house, the custom of reserving it for small children is easily understood.

The survey of 1785 describes the last of the three rooms in the Powels' back building as a "kitchen finished in the best manner," but the room that lay between this and the nursery is not further identified except for the notation that it had a cornice like that in the nursery. The only specific name applied to this middle room is found on the plan that accompanies the survey of 1859, whereon it appears as a second "kitchen." Much earlier, the Cadwaladers had thought it necessary to have two kitchens, and doubtless this intermediate room served a similar purpose for the Powels. Sometimes called "warming kitchens" or "servants' halls," rooms of this kind provided a place where the food could be kept warm while being prepared for serving and where the servants could eat and congregate while awaiting call.[63]

In estimating date and value, modern realtors and appraisers customarily look first at kitchens and bathrooms on the theory that these are the parts of a house that go out of date most quickly and that new owners are most likely to change. On this basis alone it might be assumed that the first kitchen built by Stedman had been remodeled a number of times during the past two centuries. In fact, comparison of the eighteenth-century surveys even suggests that alterations to the back building were among the numerous changes that the Powels themselves made after they purchased the house on Third Street.

Stedman advertised that the back buildings of the house he hoped to sell were "76 Feet deep," and this dimension is essentially confirmed by the "78 feet" recorded in the insurance survey made a few days after Powel purchased the house in 1769, though both measurements were doubtless intended to be only approximate. But when the Mutual Assurance Company surveyed the house fifteen years later, it found the "Back Buildings" to be only 66 feet long (Appendix I). This might easily be dismissed as an error for 76 feet were it not for the fact that a back building of approximately 66 feet, when added to a passage of about 16 feet, gives a total of 82 feet, which, in turn, corresponds closely to the total length (81.5 feet) of the back building as recorded in the survey of 1859 (Appendix II). From this it would appear that during the fifteen-year interval between the survey of the Contributionship and that of the Mutual Assurance Company the Powels had altered this part of their house as well as the important front rooms. More specifically, if we assume that the dimensions given in the advertisement and the first survey do not include the passage, it follows that the Powels must have shortened their back building by 10 to 12 feet.[64] Some support for this conclusion is found when the amount for which the Powel House was insured in 1769 is compared with that for which it was appraised in 1785; whereas the value of the main house increased by £500 during this period, that of the back building decreased by £200. Of course if the dimensions given by Stedman and in the 1769 survey are regarded as including the passage, it follows that the Powels had increased the length of the back building by about 4 to 6 feet, probably by rebuilding the large kitchen fireplace.

As it stands today, the Powel House sheds little light on this problem, since the present back building now has an exterior measurement of only about 52 feet, exclusive of the passage. At least a part of this discrepancy can be explained if it is assumed that at the west end of the back building there must once have been a large fireplace used for cooking and that sometime in the second half of the nineteenth century this was eliminated (along with part of the adjacent room) when the introduction of stoves made smaller kitchens desirable. What would seem to be a logical necessity was also confirmed in this case by shallow excavations made in 1968. These revealed the stone foundations for a hearth and chimney at a distance of about 14 feet from the end wall of the back building as presently constituted (Fig. 41).[65] Here, then, is the missing part of the back building; when added to the 52 feet of the existing structure, the additional 14 feet revealed by the excavation makes a total of 66 feet, or the exact length of the back building called

40. Back building today. By keeping the back building (or buildings) to one side of the lot, Philadelphia builders made room beside them for at least a small garden, onto which looked the windows of the back parlor.

41. Foundations of demolished west end of the back building. Under the brick of the modern patio lie the foundations of the large fireplace used for cooking in the eighteenth century. The brick wall to the left of what remains of the old chimney is part of the two-story privy that occupied the site in Isaiah Hacker's time. Photograph by Barbara Liggett.

for in the surveys of 1785 and 1859. Accordingly, this is the structure shown in the redrawn plan of the first floor of the Powel House reproduced here as Figure 21.

But if surveys and other early references offer few clues concerning the use to which were put the rooms on the first floor of the back building, they provide even less evidence of the function of the corresponding three chambers above. The wide door leading from the stair landing and the use of wainscot "surbase high" links the first of these with the front of the house and suggests that, as in the case of the "nursery" directly below, this too was intended for use by the owners. It must have been here — and presumably in the two rooms beyond — that the Powels lived when the main portion of their house was appropriated by the Earl of Carlisle during the Revolution.

Connected by a flight of tight, winding stairs to the kitchens below, the two end rooms on the upper floor of the back building would be used in later times for servants. In an era that knew no central heating, however, the furthest removed of these rooms, in particular, had the potential for being the warmest part of the house by reason of its position directly above the

main kitchen with its large open fire. Understandably, on those comparatively rare occasions when they took a winter bath, eighteenth-century Philadelphians favored this location. We know, for example, that when Washington moved to Philadelphia, he transferred to a separate building the bathing
facilities he found in this part of the Masters-Penn-Morris house in order that
he might put his own study and dressing room where they had been.[66] At
present there is no evidence to show how the Powels used this portion of
their house, but it is worth noting that in Isaiah Hacker's time one of the
upper rooms in the back building did indeed serve as a bath and contained
not only a copper-lined tub but a shower as well (Appendix II).

Most, if not all, of the doors in the back building are replacements.
Marks in the plaster showed clearly the position of the original stairs in the
northeast corner of the kitchen, however, and elsewhere this back portion
of the house appears to contain more in the way of old materials than one
might perhaps expect.[67] This may also be true of the small brick building
that now occupies the southwest corner of the garden. At least, the Hills
map, here reproduced as endpapers, shows a small structure in approximately this location. Perhaps it was originally a wash house.

The first stable, 26 by 20 feet and two stories high, apparently stood at
the west end of the original lot, where it was entered from Fourth Street. In
advertising this part of his property, Stedman noted that the foundations
were "deep enough for cellars," should the new owners wish to add living
quarters ("a tenement") above the stable. Perhaps Powel took advantage of
this opportunity, for his ledger records substantial payments "for Bricklayers
Work at my dwelling House and coach House: "£100 13 s. 11d. on August
15, 1769, and an additional £74 5s. 9d. the following March. These payments
were for labor only, and Jacob Stonematz charged a total of £84 11s. 6d. for
72,000 bricks, delivered and paid for in two installments. Substantial changes
of this kind would have required a new roof, of course, and for this Thomas
Tilbury supplied 1,700 shingles at a cost of £7 8s. 9d. Presumably all this
work was accomplished during the first fall and spring, so that by June of
1770 Fergus Purdon could pave the stable yard with cobblestones, for which
he was paid £24 10 s. 6d.

In addition to the more important back buildings that were a part of
nearly every Georgian city house, there must also have been a number of
other structures of varying sizes.[68] Most, if not all, of these have disappeared, and since they were too commonplace or taken too much for granted
to have figured prominently in the views or descriptions of the period, we
can now do little more than speculate upon their location and appearance.
In the case of the Powel House, however, it is possible that we have a picture

of such a structure, but one that has been largely overlooked, despite its inclusion in a well-known view of Philadelphia.

About 1799, when William Birch and his son Thomas engraved Bingham's mansion for inclusion in their *Philadelphia Views,* they provided at the same time our earliest extant representation of Third Street (Fig. 8). Since the Birches' view looks north, we should expect to see the Powel House in the background, but what is not so readily explained is the curious polygonal tower beside it, for which there seems to be no ready parallel in colonial Georgian architecture. The appearance of the same structure in views of the site made as late as 1817[69] eliminates the possibility that this was some kind of temporary building or perhaps even an artist's error. Whatever it was, clearly the tower was intended to be inhabited, since it has windows, and what is more, its three stories, properly defined by stone belt-courses, correspond to those of the Powel House, which significantly has no windows on the southwest corner. Moreover, photographs made shortly after the exterior of the house was restored in the 1930s show — or seem to show — the outline of this structure in the brickwork of the recently exposed south wall. This could mean either that the tower had originally abutted the main house or simply that its presence had affected the weathering of the bricks nearby.

Colonial "necessaries" (privies) were frequently polygonal in shape and until a better explanation is found, we should probably conclude that we have here one of these. As such, it was not included in the surveys of the Powel House, either because it was not yet built, because it was taken for granted, or because as a separate structure, it, like the others on the property, was not insured. If the internal design of such a structure challenges the imagination, it should be noted that in Isaiah Hacker's time at the west end of the back building there stood a two-story privy to which access at the second level was gained by means of a wooden catwalk that spanned the three feet of open passageway below. Of course, Hacker's privy was demolished long ago, but for the Bishop White House on the north side of Walnut Street near Third the National Park Service has reconstructed the kind of two-story brick one believed to have been there in the eighteenth century. And if two stories, why not three? The third story would have been desirable in this case since it appears that the principal bedrooms were at that level in Powel's time. Was this perhaps something that the Powels (or Binghams) had seen in Europe but which never became popular in Philadelphia, or is it possible that more of the Georgian mansions of Philadelphia should be thought of as having features of this kind? If it were indeed unusual, contemporary comment noting that fact ought to have survived.

To judge from insurance surveys, both the fourteen-inch brick walls of the main block of the Powel House and the nine-inch ones of the back building were standard for dwellings of its class.

Front Room Upstairs

The large room that runs the full width of the Powel House at the second level has justly been numbered among the finest interiors in America (Fig. 42). Indeed, so handsome are its proportions and so splendid its embellishments that it is tempting to follow the lead of Fiske Kimball by calling it the "Great Chamber," though it is never referred to by that name in the eighteenth-century surveys or in other contemporary comments.

It was suggested earlier that the basic plan of the Powel House derived from English sources, and from England, too, came the practice of placing the principal or state rooms on the second level, which significantly Europeans refer to as the first floor — the *piano nobile,* to use the old Italian name. Here the absence of an entrance from the outside provided maximum space, removed as far as possible from odors of street and kitchen. In the early surveys this part of the Powel House is identified simply as "the front room," and the masks and musical instruments that appear among the motifs on the plaster ceiling should probably be regarded as popular decorative devices, rather than as clues to any specific purpose for which the Powels intended this portion of their house. But even without these, or the harp and pianoforte now in the room, it requires no great effort to imagine this as the scene of the balls for which the Powels were well known. Surely it was here that Washington danced with Mrs. Sarah Franklin Bache to celebrate the birthday of her famous father, then in France.[70] Here, too, at the festivities marking her own fiftieth birthday Mrs. Powel must have danced for one of the last times before her husband's death a few months later all but ended such appearances in public; both she and M. Barbé-Marbois, the French minister, are said to have been dressed in blue satin, trimmed with squirrel skins, when they opened the ball with a minuet.[71]

Just how common was the plan of the Powel House for major Georgian dwellings in Philadelphia, it is hard to say. Since an inventory of 1786 lists a bedstead and bureau among the furnishings in the front chamber of even so rich a man as John Cadwalader,[72] this arrangement of rooms would appear to have been by no means general. But neither was it unique, to judge from the elaborate carving in the back chamber at Mount Pleasant, the house in Fairmount Park mentioned earlier, or from the second-story room wainscoted to the ceiling and ornamented with fluted pilasters described in the survey of the Byrd-Penn-Chew house, next door to the Powels' (Appendix III). Nor was the practice of placing the largest and most sumptuously decorated rooms on the second floor confined to Philadelphia. In the South we find something of the kind in notable examples like the Miles Brewton house (1765) in Charleston, South Carolina, and in Boston at the house that Charles Bulfinch (1763–1844) designed in 1795 for Harrison Gray Otis, now the headquarters of the Society for the Preservation of New England Antiquities. In Powel's case we are probably justified in seeing the importance given his front chamber as a reflection of a more sophisticated way of life acquired during his seven years abroad, and doubtless close European connections or social pretensions (or both) may usually be assumed for most colonials who favored this style of living.

There can be no doubt that the principal changes Powel made in Stedman's house were to this front room. The survey of 1769 refers to its ornamentation as being simply "the same as [that of the room] below," but the survey of 1785 describes this portion of the house as being "wainscoted to the ceiling [the only room in the house so treated] with fluted pilasters and highly ornamented." The later survey also specifically mentions the "two mahogany doors" that Powel had added and that stand in marked contrast to the simple pine ones elsewhere in the house.

Largely because of the wider boards obtainable, mahogany from the West Indies gradually supplanted walnut for the furniture and interiors of eighteenth-century buildings. In the finest Philadelphia houses of Middle Georgian date this was the material used to provide a rich accent, especially for rails, balusters, the wainscoting of stairs, and other surfaces subject to wear. The Masters-Penn-Morris house even had mahogany window sash and in the Blackwell Parlor, now at Winterthur (Fig. 65), the mantel shelf and the top of the surbase are of this material.[73] And to set them still further apart, the principal rooms of Middle Georgian houses in Philadelphia not infrequently had doors of mahogany. The Masters-Penn-Morris house had three of these and that of General Cadwalader, five.[74] It was therefore not surprising that Powel also included mahogany doors among the new embellishments of his front room. Today one of these is in the Philadelphia Museum, but its mate still serves to close the doorway between the upper passage and the large front room of the house on Third Street. The matching door in both the house and the museum is a reproduction.

In some sense, the large pilasters that flank the chimney breast of the Powels' new room may be said to echo similar elements in the lower passage (Fig. 30), and the use of the pilaster in both places should doubtless be seen against the background of the more severe classicism advocated by the neo-Palladians and discussed earlier in connection with the facade of the house. Though small pilasters occasionally flank Philadelphia overmantels of the

42. Front room upstairs, as recreated. Because it was necessary to change the location of the doors when the original was moved to the Philadelphia Museum of Art, the upstairs front room in the restored house probably gives the best impression of its appearance in Samuel Powel's time. But though perhaps correct in the general impression they convey, the decorative details of the overmantel, the carved frieze under the pediments of the doorways, the chair-rail, and the plaster frieze beneath the cornice are all as much a tribute to the ingenuity and scholarship of the restorers as to the taste and talents of the original builder and his clients.

period, extant examples of an order the full height of the room seem largely
confined to the Powel House and that begun in 1772 in Odessa, Delaware,
by William Corbit, which also — and for reasons not now entirely clear —
shares several other features with the Powel House.[75] From this it should not
be inferred, however, that the use of the large pilaster was especially unusual
when it was employed for the Powels' front room. No features of this kind
are mentioned in the descriptions of such important Philadelphia houses as
those of John Cadwalader or William Coleman,[76] but Governor Penn's front
chamber, in the house next door to the Powels', also had two fluted pilasters
(Appendix III), and the Widow Masters had no less than twelve pilasters in
the parlor of her house on High Street.[77]

Surprisingly, in describing the Powels' front room the 1785 survey does
not mention the plaster ("stucco") ceiling, which is so fine that Kimball concluded it must have been made in England.[78] Occasionally plaster ornaments
for ceilings may have been imported, but the more usual colonial practice
seems to have been to mold and carve them in place. In this case, Powel's
ledger for May of 1770 records a payment of £31 to James Clow for "stucco-
ing a ceiling." Clow, who was also responsible for the ornamented ceilings in
the Cadwaladers' house, had emigrated from England in 1763 and in Philadelphia seems to have worked closely with the carpenter-builder Robert
Smith. At least he advertised in *The Pennsylvania Journal* that he could be
reached at Smith's address on Second Street.[79]

The plant forms that comprise the decorative motifs, no less than the
light and graceful way in which they are disposed, mark the ceiling of the
Powel House as belonging to a restricted list of American interiors that show
the influence of the Rococo style (Fig. 43). In some respects a kind of final,
flamboyant manifestation of the Baroque, the Rococo first emerged as a distinctive type of French interior early in the reign of Louis XV (1715–1774).
And though by the second quarter of the eighteenth century, German and
Austrian artists had learned to apply its graceful forms and asymmetrical com-
positions with even more abandon than did their French contemporaries,
the playful Rococo remained somehow alien to the traditional British qualities of decorum and reserve. Isaac Ware, for one, condemned a ceiling,
"straggled over with arched lines and twisted curves" as "poor, fantastical
and awkward,"[80] and apart from some notable furnishings, for the interiors
of their houses British clients seem rarely to have favored the more extreme
designs in the French taste. And much the same observation might be made
concerning the few American examples of Rococo interiors that have survived. If rooms like the Blackwell Parlor (Fig. 65) appear to contradict such
generalizations, it will be noted that even here the carving is carefully con-

43. Reproduction of original plaster ceiling in the upstairs front room of the Powel House. Old photographs taken shortly after 1900 (*right*) provide assurance that both the ceiling re-installed in the Philadelphia Museum of Art and that reproduced in the Powel House are faithful to the original executed in 1770 by James Clow. The large front chamber was the only one of the Powels' rooms to be given an ornamental ceiling, and features of this kind must have been limited to the most important rooms in the finest colonial houses. At the time the Powels embellished their new house, there were at least half a dozen "plaisterers" listed on the Philadelphia tax rolls, though probably few were qualified to do ornamental work of this quality. In 1772 John Conrad provided the ornamental ceilings in John Dickinson's house.

trolled and seldom, if ever, permitted to spill over the frame, as it regularly does in the handsomest examples that serve as illustrations in the books from which American carvers drew their inspiration.

To the extent that it is made from molds taken from the original, the ceiling now in the front room of the Powel House may be considered authentic, but during 1925–26 Clow's original design was cut out and reset in a new plaster ceiling in the Philadelphia Museum, where it is rightly considered one of the major colonial achievements of the Middle Georgian period.[81] To appreciate more fully the playful qualities that distinguish its Rococo motifs, it is only necessary to compare Clow's work with two other notable Philadelphia examples that bracket it in date. Whereas the slower rhythms and heavier forms of the ceiling at Belmont (Fig. 44) belong to the earlier neo-Palladian ("Roman") style, the more restrained and geometric motifs of that on the second story of John Penn's Solitude (Fig. 45) echo the later neoclassicism made popular in England and America by the Brothers Adam.

Next to Smith, the workman listed in Powel's ledger as receiving the largest payment was Hercules Courtenay, and we may therefore assume he was probably the carver of the mantel of the front room, the most lavishly decorated part of the house as we know it today (Fig. 46). This supposition is supported by the fact that the highly ornamented portions of Cadwalader's two parlors were also entrusted to Courtenay, the gilder and carver mentioned earlier as having arrived in Philadelphia only shortly before Powel had purchased his new house. On the center panel of Cadwalader's mantel Courtenay represented the "Judgment of Hercules," but Powel's scene of the "Dog and his Shadow" from Aesop's *Fables* was probably more typical for Philadelphia at this period (Fig. 47).[82] At least half-a-dozen similar examples based on the popular *Fables* are known, and the fact that most of these are on furniture[83] is a further reminder that in many cases the same craftsmen carved both the finest Philadelphia case pieces and the most elaborate interiors. But whether on furniture or on mantels, in America such scenes seem largely confined to Georgian Philadelphia and are perhaps as near as the colonies came to producing fine sculpture in the period before the Revolution. Since the £60 paid Courtenay should have purchased more than the carving of a single panel, we may assume that the payment also included at least the trusses (brackets) that support the mantel shelf and the shell molding that surrounds the inner face, especially since Courtenay also supplied these features for the Cadwalader parlors.

At least one person who knew the old house before its woodwork had been removed recalled the Powel arms as being above the mantel in the front room, but the present cartouche, together with the entire overmantel, was designed by Fiske Kimball while director of the Philadelphia Museum of Art. The precise fate of the original is not known, but presumably it was destroyed in the late nineteenth century because it was thought a dust catcher and to make way for the wallpapers fashionable at that period.[84]

The history of the overmantel is also that of the wainscoting, which originally extended from floor to ceiling in the front chamber. Fortunately, marks left on the walls when the moldings were removed showed clearly the width and location of each, even if not the exact profile (Fig. 48).[85] Evidence of this kind also indicated that the pediments above the doors were "open,"

44. *Left.* Detail of plaster ceiling at Belmont. Used in recent years as a restaurant, Belmont was built in parts over a considerable period of time. The handsome stair is believed to date about 1760, and the third story is a Victorian addition, but the great hall with its elaborate plaster ceiling appears to have been added about 1755 by William Peters (1702–1789), attorney and loyalist. Here the arms of the Peters family figure prominently in the compartments of the decorative borders that stand in such contrast to the lighter Rococo treatment of the ceiling at the Powel House. But at Belmont are also to be noted musical instruments not unlike those featured in the central portion of the ceiling that James Clow provided for Samuel Powel. Although Isaac Ware might question the suitability of the Rococo style for ceilings, he was obliged to admit that motifs like the horn, the flute, and the hautboy could often be employed to advantage.

45. *Right.* Plaster ceiling from the library of The Solitude, Fairmount Park. In 1785 John Penn (1760–1834), grandson of William Penn, had built for himself in what are now the Zoological Gardens the delightful bachelor's retreat he named "The Solitude." The fact that Penn had but recently arrived from England may help to explain why the sophisticated disposition of their classical details — garlands, rosettes, medallions, and figures in antique dress — places the ceilings of The Solitude as close to the pure Adam style as are any to be found in America. The Adam brothers, for their part, had derived their inspiration from the antiquities brought to light in the archeological excavations begun at Pompeii and elsewhere early in the eighteenth century.

46. *Above*. Original mantel from the front room upstairs in the Powel House, now in the Philadelphia Museum of Art. Very few of the surviving colonial mantels are in a class with that of the Powels' large front chamber, but in the eighteenth century a number of the major Philadelphia houses must have had decorations that were comparable in general character and quality. Courtesy, Philadelphia Museum of Art, Gift of George D. Widener, 1926.

47. *Below*. Central panel (tablet) of the Powel mantel. Doubtless taking an engraving in one of the many editions of Aesop as a guide, the carver of the Powel mantel has shown a dog about to react to the sight of his own reflection by dropping into the water the piece of meat he is carrying in his mouth. But in the hands of Courtenay — if he were the carver, as now seems all but certain — the bridge, the trees, and even the dogs have here been transformed into a series of reciprocal curves that combine to form a delightful composition in the Rococo taste. Courtesy, Philadelphia Museum of Art, Gift of George D. Widener, 1926.

48. Southwest corner of the large front chamber of the Powel House. Photograph by Franklin D. Edmunds, 1908. Old photographs like this were a major source for the restoration of the Powels' front chamber. Here may be seen the marks left by the wainscot when it was removed, by the broken pediments that once surmounted the door frames, and by the brass escutcheon on the mahogany door. By the time of Edmund's photograph the chair-rail was also gone, but the ornamented baseboard and the cornice (without its frieze) were still in place. So, too, were the pilasters that flank the chimney breast. Later these, together with the plaster ceiling, the door frames, and the mantelpiece were acquired by the Philadelphia Museum of Art. Courtesy, Philadelphia Museum of Art.

though the carved trusses below, like the frieze between them, is an attractive but conjectural detail provided by the modern designers who recreated the room.[86] The same may be said of the "Wall-of-Troy" carving on the chair-rail ("surbase")[87] and the handsome Waterford chandelier. Though the beauty and appropriateness of the latter is undeniable, inventories — those of the most prominent Philadelphians among them — suggest that such features must have been rare in colonial America.

We are on somewhat firmer ground, however, when it comes to the cornice and skirting of the Powels' front chamber. Although both of these features had been removed by the time the Philadelphia Museum acquired the remaining woodwork in 1925,[88] the cornice had been sold in two lots,[89] one of which was ultimately installed in the Henry Francis du Pont Winterthur Museum (Fig. 49). But apparently the purchasers of the cornice did not acquire the Rococo frieze that originally had run immediately below it. Doubtless this had been stripped off and discarded much earlier, along with the overmantel and wainscoting. As restored in plaster, the present frieze was made to correspond with the profile clearly visible on the backing board to which the original had been attached (Fig. 50). A notable achievement at any time, this could probably not be duplicated today for want of craftsmen with the requisite training. If anything, re-creation of the frieze can be said to have been almost too successful; at least, carving on the pilasters and elsewhere suggests that the original was flatter and perhaps more linear than its replacement, a fact easily accounted for when it is recalled that Powel's workmen presumably carved in wood, whereas the modern restorer is known to have modeled in plasticene.[90]

When the woodwork was removed from the Powel House it was stripped of the many layers of paint that had accumulated in the course of more than a century and a half. If this did much to reveal its beauty, it also made recovery of the original colors unusually difficult. At least one of those who had a hand in removing the cornice from the front chamber later recalled that in his opinion the room had been painted a light "gray or putty color."[91] On the other hand, Kimball and his associates satisfied themselves that the more authentic color was the "cream" they finally used when the room was installed in the Philadelphia Museum.[92] If this is correct, then in Powel's time the front chamber must have presented a more somber appearance than we have come to expect in Georgian rooms of this kind. By contrast, the Cadwaladers favored such colors as blue, green, and yellow. Details in some of the Cadwaladers' principal rooms seem also to have been picked out in gold, but no specific payments for gilding have been found among Powel's accounts.[93] Perhaps Elizabeth Powel preferred to introduce color in her rooms

A

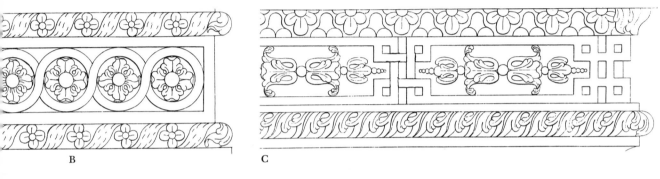

B   C

49. Original cornice from the front room upstairs in the Powel House, now in the Winterthur Museum, with two plates from the first volume of Abraham Swan's *Designs in Architecture* for comparison. At the time the large front chamber was removed from the Powel House to the Philadelphia Museum of Art, Fiske Kimball pointed out that a number of its decorative details appear to have been adapted from the plates of Abraham Swan. For example, the guilloche on the underside of the cornice (A) might well have been suggested by Plate 32 in Swan (B), while the rectilinear motif below the cornice comes close to Swan's Plate 40, though in the Philadelphia version the simpler lozenge has been substituted for the more elaborate carving of the London original (C). Courtesy, The Henry Francis du Pont Winterthur Museum.

by such devices as the crimson draperies now in the front chamber. These are made from fabric said to have been purchased by the Powels but never used.

Unlike Washington at Mount Vernon or Benjamin Chew in nearby Germantown, the Powels are not known to have taken a direct hand in developing designs for the improvements they proposed to make in their new house. To be sure, we have seen that Samuel Powel holds an architectural drawing in his portrait by Angelica Kauffmann (Fig. 2), but no Philadelphia building has been recognized from this plan and probably the artist intended it for nothing more than a compositional device or perhaps a general reference to the fact that during the eighteenth century the designing of build-

A

B

C

50. Model for the restored frieze of the front chamber in the Powel House, with several details from Swan for comparison. The photograph (A) is that sent to the Philadelphia Museum of Art by White Allom & Co. of New York to illustrate for Fiske Kimball the extent to which it had been possible to reconstruct in plasticene (at the left) and plaster (upper right) the lost frieze from the front chamber in the Powel House. Evidence used for the reconstruction included the profile visible here, which was left on the backing boards when the frieze was removed in the nineteenth century, and the plate in the second volume of Swan's *Designs in Architecture* (B) that Kimball had identified as the probable inspiration for the original frieze. Decorative details of this kind are illustrated in a number of plates in Swan; that in Plate 37, for example, includes among its motifs several of the dragons popular at the time (C). In 1770 the noted carver James Reynolds charged £2 to supply "two dragons for the pediments" in the Cadwaladers' parlor. Courtesy, Philadelphia Museum of Art and the University of Delaware Library.

ings, whether for himself or for others, was among the pastimes considered most appropriate for a gentleman.[94]

Kimball was so successful in contriving a replacement for the destroyed overmantel of Powel's front chamber because he knew in which eighteenth-century books to find the most suitable models, and historians have generally agreed that English architectural fashions made their way to the colonies primarily through illustrations in architectural books. It is not difficult to imagine the Powels looking for details that appealed to them in some of these — perhaps even in one or more of the "Sundry Books of Architecture" mentioned but not named in the inventory of Robert Smith's estate. Certainly the frieze of Powel's front chamber appears to have been not unlike several plates in the second volume of Abraham Swan's *Designs in Architecture* (Fig. 50), and from the same source may come the fret design (Fig. 51) used for the baseboard.

Occasionally, as here, a craftsman might borrow single details more or less directly from his English source, but the freedom with which motifs are handled in the cornice of the same room (Fig. 49), where a simple lozenge is substituted for the more complicated ornament of the original,[95] is more typical of Philadelphia practice. Elsewhere in the colonies, the design of a complete chimney breast or for a whole facade might occasionally be lifted more or less intact from such books as those by Swan or Gibbs,[96] but no examples of such direct borrowing on a large scale are known in Philadelphia. Why this should be so has never been satisfactorily explained; perhaps it was because, as the most artistically sophisticated of American cities, colonial Philadelphia attracted more accomplished craftsmen than did its neighbors to the north and south. It is therefore not surprising that as yet no single source has been found for the design of any of the principal elements of the Powels' front room; almost certainly none exists.

Back Room Upstairs

Apart from the entrance passage, the only major portion of the Powel House to survive intact into the twentieth century is the back room at the second level (Fig. 52), and as such it has already been mentioned as the model used in re-creating the two principal rooms on the floor below. At the time the Metropolitan Museum of Art acquired it in 1917, the back room was described by one of those who recommended its purchase as being "in pretty good shape, except the paint which [had] cracked and scaled,"[97] a judgment that is well supported by photographs made earlier in the twentieth century.

As in the case of most of the other rooms, contemporary references offer few clues to the specific uses that occupants of the Powel House made of this one. It is not referred to by name in the survey of 1769, and that of 1785 notes only that the "second story back room [is] the same as below." Those who danced in the front room nearby would have required refreshment, of course, and perhaps it was here that its owners used the large covered punch bowl said to have been a gift from General Cadwalader and now in the Metropolitan Museum (Fig. 53). Here, too, we can easily imagine the Powels and their guests as playing cards, a pastime that took a variety of forms and one in which well-to-do colonials took such delight that they followed the lead of their English cousins in demanding splendid mahogany tables especially designed for the purpose.

51. Original skirting (baseboard) from the front room upstairs in the Powel House, now in the Winterthur Museum. Since Philadelphia craftsmen rarely followed their English models exactly, the closeness of the decorative treatment of the baseboard in the Powels' large front chamber (*above*) to Plate 30 in *Designs in Architecture* (*below*) helps to explain Fiske Kimball's emphasis on the importance of Abraham Swan as a major influence on Philadelphia architectural design in the Middle Georgian period. Significantly, Swan's were the first English architectural books to be brought out in America, and Philadelphia was the place of publication. New printings of *The British Architect* (1st ed., London, 1745) and *A Collection of Designs in Architecture* (1st ed., London, 1757) were undertaken by John Norman in 1775, though of course through private and institutional libraries both books had been available in Philadelphia well before that date. Courtesy, The Henry Francis du Pont Winterthur Museum.

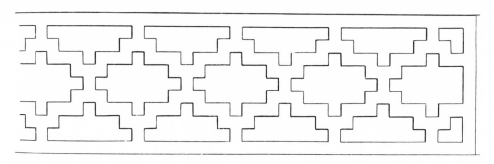

52. Back room upstairs in the Powel House. As now installed in the house on South Third Street, this room reproduces the original that since 1917–18 has been part of the American Wing in the Metropolitan Museum of Art. Here the cornice has a fret design instead of the dentils used in the room below, though in other respects the two rooms are described in the insurance surveys as being similar. These door frames also lack the "knees" (sometimes called "crossettes" or, less elegantly, simply "dog ears") of the lower room, suggesting that originally the Stedmans intended a less important role for this part of their house than was subsequently assigned it by the Powels.

53. Large punch bowl with cover and platter. Made in China for the Western market about 1750. The decoration is believed to depict scenes in the Dutch East Indies. In the 1931 exhibit of Powel furnishings at the Philadelphia Museum of Art this bowl was listed as having been a gift to the Powels, and certainly in date and quality it is illustrative of the pieces that must once have filled their house on Third Street. Courtesy, The Metropolitan Museum of Art, Pulitzer Fund, 1940.

Less conjectural than the function served by the rear room is the source of the design for its chimneypiece (Fig. 54). Though suggestive parallels may be found in the books of Swan and others, in point of fact we need look no further afield than the customary practices of the Carpenters' Company. Stripped of the decorative details, the chimneypiece illustrated in the company's *Articles and Rules* (Fig. 55) is remarkably close to that in the Powel House. Pressed for funds wherewith to complete his house, Stedman presumably limited himself to the basic Georgian design recommended by the Carpenters' Company, omitting as unnecessary expense the carved scrolls that flank the "landscape panel" in Plate XXVII. A plain chimneypiece of this kind would not have satisfied the Powels, however, especially in a location near the front room they had engaged Courtenay and others to embellish so richly. And since both the carved trusses that support the mantel shelf and the fretwork that ornaments the broken pediment echo similar details on the new mantel added to the front chamber (Fig. 46), doubtless these features — as well as the carving in the "knees" of the architrave and on the "tablet" beneath the mantel shelf — should be considered as among the additions that Powel made to his back chamber shortly after he acquired the house from Stedman.[98]

Chambers at the Third Level

The two large chambers at the third level of the Powel House were apparently used as family bedrooms. Evidence of this may be found in the mahogany stair that continues uninterrupted from the second level. Though it has a window, the third room would have been limited in its usefulness by its small size and by the absence of a chimney wherewith to heat it. Possibly it was intended principally for storage.

The surveys of 1769 and 1785 describe the third story as being simply finished with paneled chimney breasts, chair-rails ("surbases"), baseboards (skirting), and a cornice,[99] and this conforms essentially to their appearance today. The finish of the two principal rooms also matches the description of those which in 1926 the Philadelphia Museum listed as being given by Mr. and Mrs. Wolf Klebansky and which were presumably returned when the Landmarks Society undertook to restore the house. Though neither the insurance surveys nor the museum records mention the tiles that now surround the fireplace of the west room (Fig. 56), in a 1917 letter to the Metropolitan Museum, Alfred C. Prime, the antiquarian, mentioned "some Dutch tiles from a fireplace on the third floor." This suggests that if these we now see were not there in the Powels' time, tiles of some kind probably surrounded one or both of the upper-chamber fireplaces in the eighteenth century.

In recent years the need to make structural repairs in the bedchambers has served to reveal details of the framing of the Powel House that could otherwise have escaped notice. Ordinarily, one might have expected the builders to run the floor joists from front to rear of the main rooms in order that one end could be supported on the brick wall that bisects the house and extends from cellar to garret. This would have required joists about twenty feet long, however, and apparently colonial builders in Philadelphia considered lengths greater than about seventeen feet to be inefficient and uneconomical in situations of this kind. In the Powel House this optimum length is made possible by running the joists from side to side (north and south) and by supporting them at mid-point by a large girder, which on each

54. Chimneypiece from the back room upstairs in the Powel House. Now installed in the American Wing of the Metropolitan Museum of Art. Original in all but minor details, this served as the model when similar features had to be restored in both the principal rooms on the ground floor of the Powel House. The general design was a simple one popular in the Philadelphia area, but the carved details were doubtless among the decorations contributed by some of the prominent craftsmen whom Samuel Powel engaged to embellish further the house he had recently purchased from Charles Stedman. Photograph by Jay Cantor. Courtesy, The Metropolitan Museum of Art.

XXVII

55. Plate XXVII from the *Articles and Rules* of the Carpenters' Company of the City and County of Philadelphia. Like most organizations of its kind, the Carpenters' Company relinquished slowly its earlier practices and traditions. Though originally published in 1786, this design of a chimneypiece makes no concessions to the lighter and more graceful forms of the Late Georgian style then coming into favor. Probably it represents fairly accurately the prevailing taste during the decades immediately preceding the Revolution, when were built many of the greatest Philadelphia houses, including that of Samuel Powel. In fact, the plate in the *Articles and Rules* probably stands closer to the chimneypiece in the large front chamber of William Corbit's house in Odessa, Delaware (installed about 1774) than does the corresponding feature in the Powels' rear chamber (Fig. 54), sometimes cited as having been Corbit's model.

56. West chamber at the third level of the Powel House. The comparatively simple treatment accorded both the Powels' upper chambers was characteristic of even the finest Middle Georgian houses in Philadelphia. Identical decoration in similar rooms of Alexander Stedman's house and in the Byrd-Penn-Chew house next door to the Powels' was perhaps to be expected, but the upper chambers in even the Masters-Penn-Morris house — mentioned elsewhere as perhaps the finest in the city — are described as having only "chimney Brests, Surbass [chair-rail] & Scertings [baseboard]." As here, there must also have been a single or double cornice, which the surveyor neglected to mention.

of the three principal floors lies several feet inside (i.e., south of) the partition shared with the passage (Fig. 57). This partition is of light frame construction and is found only on the first and third levels; in the cellar it was

57. Floor construction at the third level of the Powel House. Massive timbers that support the floor beams (joists) were usually called "summers" in New England but "girders" in Philadelphia. Girders like this one run from front to rear in the two principal rooms on each of the three levels of the Powel House. To hold the joists in place, a projecting flange (tenon) at the end of each was made to fit a cavity (mortis) cut in the girder and secured there by means of a large wooden peg (treenail). Tenons with "double tusking" were stronger — and also more expensive — than the single variety. This system of framing had the further advantage of bringing either a girder or a series of joists into contact with each of the four exterior walls, thereby contributing to the rigidity and stability of the whole fabric.

unnecessary, and at the second level it had perforce to be omitted by reason of the large room that occupies the full width of the house at that point. Only for the floor of the garret do the joists run from front to rear. This practice was customary in order that the ends of the joists might help support the exterior cornice on the facade and rear of the house, while at the same time tying into the sloping rafters of the roof to form a triangular truss.

The girders appear to do their job well enough at the first and second levels, but possibly because they feared any vibration would damage the elaborate plaster ceiling below, the builders added at the third level a substantial truss (Fig. 58) like that illustrated in the *Articles and Rules* of the Carpenters' Company and now largely concealed behind plaster walls. Perhaps to this precaution we owe in part the excellent condition in which Clow's ceiling has survived into the twentieth century.

Garret

Now partitioned into one small room and two larger ones, the garret of the Powel House has plastered walls and is so described in the survey of 1769. Here probably slept the servants, including perhaps some of the household slaves the Powels are known to have owned.[100]

Furnishings

The preceding discussion of individual rooms included a few comments concerning their probable appointments, but unless a detailed inventory is found there is no way of knowing the full extent of the early furnishings of the Powel House or much concerning their arrangement.[101] We can be certain, however, that eighteenth-century rooms were furnished quite differently from those found today in most museums and historic houses. For one thing, old prints — most of them English, to be sure — suggest that chairs and tables were usually placed against the wall and only brought out into the room when in use. And since a good case can be made that "easy chairs" were intended primarily for the aged or the ill, they were more likely to be found in the chambers than in the parlor. In short, the familiar fireside group of upholstered chair with candlestand or tea table beside it is an appealing invention of the modern decorator for which little or no historic precedent can be found.

In relating some of the details of his sojourn in Philadelphia, the Marquis de Chastellux recalled that the Powels had a "handsome house furnished in the English manner and . . . adorned with fine prints and some very good copies of the best Italian paintings"; the latter he implied were brought back by the owner from his European travels, in the course of which he had

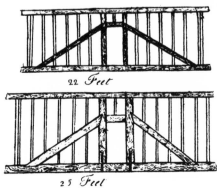

22 *Feet*

25 *Feet*

58. Wall truss at the third level of the Powel House. As reproduced here for comparison, Plate XV of the *Articles and Rules* of the Carpenters' Company illustrated two similar wall trusses that might be used when the weight on the floor was expected to be unusually heavy or when there was insufficient support below. The lower of the two engravings also shows the use of iron straps or braces similar to those found in the Powel House. Exposed timbers of this kind are so commonplace in late seventeenth-century construction in New England that it is not always remembered that in concealed form they are also to be found throughout the Georgian period and even in brick buildings such as those favored in Philadelphia.

"acquired a taste for the fine arts."[102] If so, none of the prints or copies referred to by the Marquis have been identified, unless it be the three paintings on velvet now in the front room of the ground floor. These are said to have once belonged to Powel and certainly they seem the kind of thing a young colonial traveling in Europe might have been tempted to buy. To these putative mementos of the Grand Tour should perhaps be added two neoclassical vases on marble stands that have descended in the Powel family and that are currently on display in the front room. These and other furnishings with a Powel history that have been given to the Landmarks Society are listed in Appendix IV.

Again using prints as a guide, we can interpret Chastellux's comments, quoted above, to mean that in at least some of the Powels' rooms pictures may have been so numerous they had to be hung in rows, one above the other, with perhaps even one or two over the doorways. None of the prints owned by the Powels have been identified, but a number of their most important paintings were mentioned earlier: Pratt's portraits of Mrs. Powel (Figs. 4 and 7), Wright's portrait of General Washington (Fig. 6), and Angelica Kauffmann's portraits of Powel (Fig. 2) and of herself (Fig. 1). Despite the fact it was never finished, Pratt's painting of Mrs. Powel that was later erroneously attributed to Gilbert Stuart may also have hung in the house on Third Street. Taken together, these portraits form the largest category of Powel furnishings about which we can be certain. To them should perhaps be added a hypothetical "landskip" or two above one or more of the mantels, after the fashion of the period.

What we call "mirrors," and the eighteenth century termed "looking glasses," would have figured prominently in the furnishings of any major city house, and we know that those of the Powels' included the oval pair of gilded Hepplewhite ones received from General Washington when a span of horses bought from him proved faulty.[103] In fact, no major eighteenth-century house in Philadelphia could be considered well appointed that did not include at least one of the elaborate mahogany and gilt looking glasses intended primarily to decorate the areas (piers) between the symmetrically placed windows that had become so prominent a feature of the facades of Georgian houses.

Through the generosity of a member of the Powel family, a number of Samuel Powel's books have been returned to his house in recent years. To hold these and other volumes, some of which had doubtless been acquired abroad, there would have had to be one or more bookcases.[104] Clocks would also have been a necessity, and among those which Edward Duffield and John Nood cleaned and repaired may well have been the tall one now in the

Metropolitan Museum (Fig. 59), which is said to have been acquired from a collateral descendant. In the eighteenth century the stair landing seems to have been a favorite place for clocks of this kind.

59. Tall clock. Works by William Huston of Philadelphia (fl. 1770–1785). As among the most Baroque features used in the colonies, the swan's-neck pediment early appeared in the architecture of the south, and was favored in certain parts of New England until well into the nineteenth century, but in Philadelphia its use seems to be confined to important pieces of furniture. Standing almost nine feet high, this great clock was acquired from a collateral descendant of the Powels. Courtesy, The Metropolitan Museum of Art, Morris K. Jesup Fund, 1948.

In addition to a variety of tables and chairs, other furnishing we can be certain the Powels must have owned would include at least one desk,[105] a sofa or a settee — perhaps several — and of course a number of the chests of drawers that were made in various forms and sizes and for which eighteenth-century craftsmen are justly noted. Both the high chest and double chest (chest-on-chest) were popular in Georgian Philadelphia, though the lower type was made in greater numbers. That reproduced as Figure 60 has been attributed to Jonathan Gostelowe (1745–1795) and is of special interest here because of its Powel history. In later times, changing customs led to the practice of placing such important case pieces in the principal rooms of the house in order that they might be seen to advantage. When originally made, however, they were intended primarily for use in chambers, where, in the absence of closets, they were used to hold articles of clothing.

At present we know nothing about the beds the Powels must have owned, but as hung with yards of rich material, fringed and betasseled, these may well have been among the most notable furnishings in the house. Chippendale devoted over a dozen of the plates in the third edition of his *Director* (London, 1762) to illustrating beds with carved Rococo canopies in the "Gothick" or French taste. Perhaps such an engraving provided the inspiration for the bed ordered by John Cadwalader in 1771. As described by Wainwright, the festoons, plumes, and laces with which this was decorated by the upholsterer Plunket Fleeson must indeed have made it an object of "almost barbaric splendor." Powel's bed may not have been so grand as Cadwalader's, but it was undoubtedly impressive, nonetheless.

From Powel's ledger we learn also of a pair of brass firedogs bought from Daniel King and another acquired from Samuel Grove, who also provided material for "mosketo curtains." Other brass items supplied by King included a pair of candlesticks.

More important than the identification of individual items, however, is the larger question of the ratio of American artifacts to those imported from Europe among the total furnishings of the house during the Powels' occupancy. Chastellux's comment that the furnishings were "in the English manner" is of little help in this respect, inasmuch as no one but an expert could hope to distinguish the best Philadelphia pieces from their English prototypes. The boycott of English goods prevailing during much of the 1760s obliged patriotic Philadelphians like Cadwalader to patronize Philadelphia craftsmen, but significantly a number of the Powel furnishings exhibited at the Philadelphia Museum in 1931 were English,[106] and under ordinary circumstances most well-to-do colonials doubtless preferred goods of European manufacture to those produced locally.

60. Mahogany chest of drawers. Pennsylvania, c. 1765–1775. Pieces of this kind came in a variety of sizes; this one measures 36 in. by 42½ in. by 24 in., and in general form must resemble the walnut chest with "fluted Cullums & Swell'd Brackets" for which William Savery charged John Cadwalader £11 in 1770. The quarter columns at the corners are a reminder of the close relationship that existed between architecture and cabinet making during the eighteenth century. Several of the craftsmen who embellished the interiors of the Cadwaladers' house also supplied some of their furnishings, and it will be recalled that Thomas Chippendale began his popular *Director* by illustrating and describing the five orders. Courtesy, Mrs. Lydia Bond Powel.

To forestall any plan his nephew might have to order numerous furnishings while in London, Powel's uncle, who was also his agent in America, had cautioned:

> Household goods may be had here as cheap and as well made from English patterns. In the humour people are in here, a man is in danger of becoming Invidiously distinguished, who buys anything in England which our Tradesmen can furnish. I have heard the joiners here object this against Dr. Morgan & others who brought their furnishings with them.[107]

Apparently advice of this kind did not completely discourage young Powel, however. While still abroad he wrote to ask that his uncle be certain the porters engaged to unload the goods he was sending "be very careful lest any damage should happen to them,"[108] and after his return Powel's ledger lists at least one payment for "Freight of furniture from London." This was in March of 1771 and possibly covered items not readily available in Philadelphia.

The fact that Samuel and Elizabeth Powel came from prominent families has already been noted, and doubtless both received numerous household furnishings as gifts and through inheritance. A few references to possessions of earlier generations of the Powel family have come to light, but we can only speculate concerning which of these might have found its way into the house on Third Street. Because another is at Winterthur,[109] the impressive walnut armchair now in the Philadelphia Museum (Fig. 61) must have been one of a pair or perhaps even part of a set, possibly a large one. Record of its association with an earlier generation of Powels goes back no further than William Macpherson Hornor, Jr.,[110] but if this chair be considered a reliable indication of their character, the older pieces of Powel furniture must have been of the highest quality. Perhaps this explains why the third Samuel Powel's ledger contains so few references to items of this kind. In fact, the only major Philadelphia cabinetmaker to whom he seems to have given an order was William Savery (1721–1788), and the 4s. 6d. paid him on December 10, 1770, would have bought only the simplest type of "child's chair." Possibly it was similar to the one said to have been made for Powel's nephew, Samuel Powel Griffitts (1759–1826), and now owned by his descendants (Fig. 62). As it turned out, the deaths in infancy of the Powels' two sons meant that even Savery's chair would be of little use to them.

But no matter how affluent, few persons can expect to have everything needed to furnish a new house. Predictably, the Powels' floor coverings proved either insufficient or the wrong size. James Fisher was accordingly

61. *Left*. Walnut "Queen Anne" armchair. Philadelphia, c. 1740–1750. In his catalog of the Winterthur collection, Joseph Downs described the mate to this chair as having features characteristic of the highest development of mid-eighteenth-century colonial craftsmanship. In view of its quality and probable date before 1750, it is tempting to believe that the chair was made for Samuel Powel, the merchant, or possibly for his father, the "rich carpenter," and later used by the son or grandson in his house on South Third Street. If Mayor Powel did not own this chair, he doubtless owned some like it. Courtesy, Philadelphia Museum of Art, The Harrison Fund, 1955.

62. *Right*. Child's high chair. Believed to have been made in Philadelphia about 1760 for use by Samuel Powel Griffitts. Since young Griffitts would have been eleven years old in 1770, this cannot be the chair Samuel Powel ordered from William Savery in that year, but it may well resemble it. Probably pieces of this kind were fairly well standardized by Savery; at least in 1771 he also made John Cadwalader a child's chair for 4s. 6d., the same price he charged Powel. It now seems clear, in fact, that some of the most important Philadelphia shops were turning out extremely simple furniture at the same time they were making the high-style pieces for which they are best known. Thus, for the John Cadwaladers, Savery made not only a number of walnut pieces for use in their bedchambers but also, and at the same time, tables and chairs for their kitchen. Courtesy, John A. Ballard.

paid £13 14s. for forty-four yards of carpeting; William Adcock received £4 10s. for "two Ruggs," otherwise unidentified, and William Turner provided "a Green Rug" for £1 15s. Probably Fisher furnished "Scotch" carpet, since the amount paid him would not have been sufficient to buy the Wilton carpeting popular in Philadelphia at this period.[111] Neither in Powel's accounts nor in other contemporary records is there much to show the purchase in quantity of the handsome carpets from the Near East understandably favored by those charged with furnishing period rooms in museums and historic houses.

Old fabrics must also have seemed unsuited to new surroundings. On September 30, 1769, Susannah Bond received £2 15s. 10d. "for upholsterer's work" and from time to time during the early 1770s John Webster was paid considerable sums for "sundry upholstery." Webster advertised himself as an upholsterer from London who, in addition to hanging rooms with "paper, chintz, damask or tapestry," stood ready to install the "newest invented Venetian sun blinds,"[112] presumably the kind the Powels purchased in March of 1770. He also offered for sale "Webster's Liquor," a formula "for entirely destroying that offensive and destructive vermin called Buggs," though there is no record the Powels found it necessary to include this among their purchases.

From Joseph Stansbury the Powels bought new china of an unnamed kind, and to Alexander Bartram they paid £4 2s. 10d. for "Queen's Ware," a type of earthenware the latter advertised as being for sale at his shop on High Street.[113] The blue and white Nanking pieces on view in what is now furnished as a dining parlor have been lent to the Powel House by the Mount Vernon Ladies' Association of the Union as a portion of the dinner service given to Mrs. Powel by General Washington, but the French china displayed in the buffet is said to have been a gift from Powel to his wife. Shortly after purchasing Stedman's house the Powels also paid Mifflin and Dean £2 17s. 6d. for "Japanned [i.e. painted] wares."

With their silver claw-and-ball feet and finely wrought mounts of the same material, the pair of knife boxes (Fig. 63) now on display in the downstairs back room of the Powel House are superb examples of their kind and eloquent testimony to the high quality of English furnishings imported by prominent Philadelphians during the eighteenth century. It is easy to accept these as having been among the appointments of his house on Third Street during Samuel Powel's lifetime, but we cannot be sure, of course, that some articles that have descended in the Powel family were not acquired for use at Powelton or at one of Mrs. Powel's later houses. This would be true, for example, of the mahogany fire screen and the cellarette now in the house;

63. One of a pair of mahogany knife boxes. English c. 1760–1770. Items of this kind were popular with colonists of means. In 1769 John Cadwalader imported from London a pair of such cases, "lined & laced with silver & ornamented with silver furniture." Cadwalader's boxes were made by Henry Shepherd, but this and its mate are marked "IW" and were given to the Landmarks Society as part of the furnishings that had descended in the Powel family.

both have a Powel history but neither can be dated much earlier than the end of the eighteenth century.

The exhibit of the Powel furnishings held at the Philadelphia Museum in 1931 included twenty-eight pieces of American and English silver, among them parts of the dinner service made for Elizabeth Powel by Richard Humphrey, the noted Philadelphia silversmith. Described in the account of the exhibition as being plain except for a molded serpentine edge, the Humphrey silver must match the pair of oval dishes now owned by the Philadelphia Museum (Fig. 64). These are marked with the Powel crest but in this case are the work of Joseph Richardson, Jr. (1752–1831), another of Philadelphia's most celebrated craftsmen.[114] Shortly after their marriage, the Powels also purchased additional spoons from Philip Syng, Jr., a silversmith best known as the maker of the inkstand that served the Speaker of the Pennsylvania Assembly and therefore presumably the signers of both the Declaration of Independence and the Constitution, as well.

Despite the comparatively small number of Powel furnishings that have thus far come to light, the understated elegance of the Richardson silver combines with the vigorous lines of the Queen Anne armchair and the dignified restraint of the "Gostelowe" chest of drawers to provide a glimpse of a quality of life that helped to distinguish Philadelphia among the major cities of colonial America.

Garden

Powel's garden was considerably larger than the one we see today; not only did his lot extend the full distance to Fourth Street, but a month after he purchased the property from Stedman, he acquired an additional thirty feet on Third Street from Dr. William Smith, provost of the College of Philadelphia.[115] This would have provided a ninety-foot front, instead of the present sixty-foot one, but beyond this fact and a few other miscellaneous details, little is known that would help us to visualize the appearance of the garden in the eighteenth century.

To ensure privacy there was presumably a brick wall along Third Street, and this — or at least the gate — was capped by the stone balls Powel bought in 1770. Cadwalader's gate was similarly ornamented, but in place of the stone wall topped by iron spikes that protected the other sides of Cadwalader's garden, Powel probably contented himself with the wooden fence that in 1770 James Barnes painted for the considerable sum of £23 4s. 1d.

The trees and other plants for which Jacob Walter was paid £8 19s. in 1770 are not named, but the next year the same supplier provided a buttonwood (sycamore) tree. Either this died or Powel liked it so well he wanted

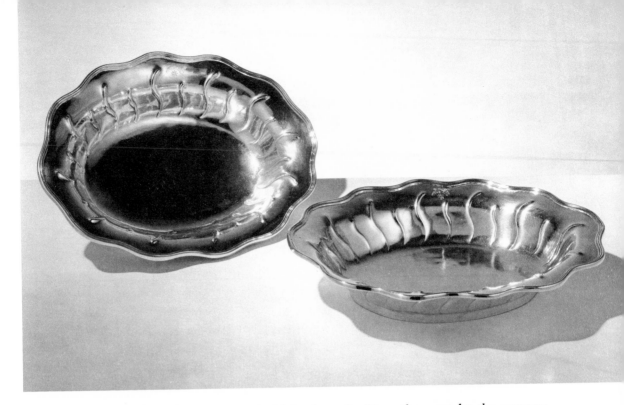

64. Pair of silver dishes. Made by Joseph Richardson, Jr. Since these are by the younger Richardson, they may date as late as 1800 and therefore after the death of Samuel Powel. The crest makes certain the identification with the Powel family, however, and their simple but effective design must have been made to conform to earlier pieces of Mrs. Powel's silver. They are eleven inches in diameter. Courtesy, Philadelphia Museum of Art, The McIlhenny Fund, 1956.

another, for a year later Walter billed him 15s. "for a Button Wood & poplar Trees." Possibly it was these the Contributionship considered so much a fire hazard that Powel was obliged to transfer his insurance to the Mutual Assurance Company, as noted earlier.

From time to time Powel paid men with such names as Fling, Spring, and Cummins to work in his garden, and for some reason considerable amounts of earth had to be hauled away. This may have been connected with improvements in the cellars, or perhaps had something to do with the kitchen garden, where, among other vegetables, the Powels grew cabbage and asparagus.

In the course of preparing animal hair for sale, Wolf Klebansky had erected a factory of sorts to the rear of the main house, and this had obliterated any trace that might have remained of the original garden. Once this was removed, a new garden was planted, and this, in turn, was redesigned during the 1950s.[116] Confined to plants known to have been available in the eighteenth century, the present design may well capture something of the spirit of the original, though it must necessarily remain conjectural in its details.

Reappraisal

Sumptuous as it undoubtedly was, Powel's was by no means the most lavishly ornamented of the Middle Georgian houses in Philadelphia, as has occasionally been suggested. When quartered there, the Earl of Carlisle correctly described it simply as "one of the best . . . in the town . . . indeed . . . a very excellent one, perfectly well furnished,"[117] and significantly Lord Howe preferred as his headquarters the house built by Mary Lawrence Masters on High Street. Apparently the British commander chose wisely; a few years later, the Masters house (then owned by Robert Morris) was again selected as being most appropriate for use by both Presidents Washington and Adams during the period when Philadelphia served as the temporary capital of the country.

One reason for preferring the Masters-Penn-Morris house as an official residence was its greater size, but surveys and records of payments to their workmen by Cadwalader and others also make clear that at least in the finishing of some of their rooms the owners of a number of Philadelphia houses went appreciably beyond anything attempted by the Powels. Visual proof of this may also be found in the surviving portions of the Pine Street house once occupied by the Reverend Robert Blackwell, the doorway of which was mentioned earlier (Fig. 28). Now installed in the Henry Francis du Pont Winterthur Museum and furnished with some of the finest examples of Philadelphia craftsmanship, the Blackwell Parlor (Fig. 65) is considerably more elaborate in its ornamentation than are any of the other rooms illustrated here. Whereas Powel's mantel is decorated with a single scene, that of Blackwell has no less than three,[118] and similar differences are to be noted when the cornices or other details of the two rooms are compared. Though there are no other extant Philadelphia houses with which Powel's can readily be compared, the similarity of its features to those illustrated in the *Articles and Rules* of the Carpenters' Company suggests that, except possibly for the importance given the front chamber, it should be regarded as fairly typical of its class. In fact, it was precisely this relative simplicity that doubtless made the Powel House attractive to the Delaware tanner William Corbit as a model for his own dwelling at Odessa, noted previously.

In seeking to preserve an important house on its original site, Miss Wister and her associates may be said to have more nearly resembled later preservationists than a majority of their contemporaries, most of whom were

65. Blackwell Parlor. Downstairs front room removed early in the twentieth century from the house said to have been built about 1764 at 224 Pine Street. Presumably this was the most elaborately decorated room in the Reverend Robert Blackwell's residence. Certainly it is the most highly ornamented Philadelphia interior to survive from the Middle Georgian or any other period, and its installation in the Winterthur Museum makes it possible to view the embellishments of the Powel House in better perspective. Courtesy, The Henry Francis du Pont Winterthur Museum.

still engaged in moving a variety of old buildings to create quaint villages of their own conception or in adapting woodwork from old houses to form backgrounds for the notable collections of American furnishings then being assembled by major museums and a number of private collectors. According to the generally accepted view of that day, when the original room was not judged suitable for its new function, it might be enlarged, reduced, or combined with another to meet the altered requirements. In this way, doors and windows could be added to suit the new owner's convenience; if the original style were judged too simple, more elaborate features were often borrowed from another source; when the original color did not complement a favorite rug or picture, another was adopted. But no matter what the changes, the objective was always the creation of a work of art; and in the hands of talented architects and designers, these practices frequently produced rooms of remarkable beauty and distinction, whatever historical violence may have been done to the period they were more less intended to interpret.

It would be hard to read the correspondence relating to the restoration and preservation of the Powel House without being impressed by the care and scholarly imagination with which those in charge approached their exacting task. If the foregoing discussion has contained mention of some of the historical guesses and architectural liberties made or taken by architects like Fiske Kimball and Louis Duhring, it was partly in the interests of historical accuracy and partly because it should be recognized that, like any other restoration, the Powel House is not only a monument to the period that first built it, but also in some degree to the period that preserved it. As with most forms of human activity, historic preservation has been subject to a continuing evolution, which may now be said to have a history of its own.[119] The Powel House figures importantly in this history, and though a later and more pedantic age may be inclined to judge restored buildings on the basis of their "authenticity," it is by no means certain that it would be wise to eliminate the creative touches provided by earlier scholar-architects such as Kimball and Duhring. After nearly a half-century they may be said to possess a kind of historic value in their own right.

Nor should it be supposed that in the development of standards for historic preservation the last word has yet been spoken. With the two earlier periods represented by the Powel House, mention should also be made of a third: whereas preservationists of the 1920s may be said to have concerned themselves largely with rooms or fragments of rooms and those of the 1930s with the individual structure, in the decades following World War II attention has been increasingly directed to the larger area of the neighborhood.

The return of even a single block of Third Street to its appearance in Powel's time would, of course, be impractical, assuming it were desirable. In their attempt to provide an environment that would meet the needs of the twentieth century while still respecting the heritage of the colonial past, the several Philadelphia agencies responsible for planning and preservation declined to save the imaginative but highly individual facade that Wilson Eyre, Jr., (1858–1944) had added about 1881 a few yards to the north of the Powel House, though at the same time they were willing to accept a half-block of modern town houses designed by I. M. Pei directly opposite. Predictably, neither of these decisions has met with the unanimous approval of either laymen or specialists — a reminder of how elusive are acceptable standards in this field and of how difficult it is to practice the art of historic preservation amid the demands of contemporary society.

Appendix I

EIGHTEENTH-CENTURY INSURANCE SURVEYS

FOR THE POWEL HOUSE

Below in parallel columns for easy comparison are listed the principal features of the Powel House as described in the surveys of the Philadelphia Contributionship (No. 1342–44; August 26, 1769) and the Mutual Assurance Company (No. 39–42; January 11, 1785). It should be borne in mind that the two surveys were not only made at different times but also by different men: Gunning Bedford for the Contributionship; Isaac Jones for the Mutual Assurance Company. Most of the spellings have been modernized.

	1769 Survey	*1785 Survey*
MAIN HOUSE		
General Description	front 30 ft.	[front] 31 ft.
	depth 46 ft.	[depth] 45 ft.
	3 stories; 2 rooms and a passage on each story	
	exterior walls 14 in. thick	walls 14 in. thick
	interior walls 9 in. thick	
	painted inside and out	
Facade	"modillion eaves"	"modillion eaves"
First Story Passage	wainscot "pedestal high,"* cornice of dentils [2] "fluted pilasters with an arch"	"wainscoted surbase high and highly ornamented"

	1769 Survey	*1785 Survey*
	pediments over doors doweled floor	[this area now called "hall"]
Stairs	"2 stories of open newel stairs, ramped, bracketed, and wainscoted . . . with a twist"; one story mahogany	"rampt and twist mahogany stairs wainscoted with mahogany two stories"
Front Room	wainscot "pedestal high,"* dentil cornice "all round" [full wainscoting] and tabernacle frame on chimney breast pediments over doors	"finished in the same style" [as back room]
Back Room	same as front room	"wainscoted surbase"* dentil cornice "round the room" mantel [with] tabernacle frame [above] 2 pediments "windows cased with architraves round"
Second Story		
Passage	same as first floor except for doweled floor, [2 pilasters] and arch	
Front Room	"same as below"	"wainscoted to the ceiling with fluted pilasters and highly ornamented" "2 mahogany doors"
Back Room	"same as below"	"same as below"
Third Story		
Front Chamber	[wainscot on] chimney breast surbase skirting** single cornice	plain [chimney] breasts surbase washboards "single cornice round the room" "windows cased"

	1769 Survey	*1785 Survey*
Back Chamber	same as front chamber	[same as front chamber]
Garret	plastered and with partitions	
BACK BUILDING(S)	78 ft. by 16 ft. 2 stories 9 in. walls "3 rooms on a floor" painted inside and out	66 ft. by 14 ft. 2 stories high 9 in. walls
First Story		
Front Room		"wainscoted surbase high" cornice round [this room now called "nursery"]
Middle Room		cornice round
Rear Room		"finished in the best manner" [called "kitchen"]
Second Story		
Front Chamber		"wainscoted surbase high"
Middle Chamber		"plain [chimney] breast and cornice"
Rear Chamber		"plain [chimney] breast and cornice"

"about 4 years old"

"two small trees before the door and several in the garden."

Bedford approved
£1,000 on the house
and £500 on the back
building

Jones approved
£1,500 on the house
and £300 on the back
building

* The phrases "pedestal high" and "surbase high" are interchangeable; both mean wainscoting only below what today would probably be called a chair-rail.

** The term "skirting" is interchangeable with "washboard" and both are similar to the modern baseboard.

Appendix II

1859 INSURANCE SURVEY

FOR THE POWEL HOUSE

Survey (No. 10.224) of the Powel House for the Philadelphia Contributionship, May 14, 1859 (punctuation added).

I have Surveyed a Brick Building used as Offices belonging to Isaiah Hacker situate on the West side of Third Street between Spruce and Walnut streets (No. 258). The Main Building being 30 feet Front by 46 feet deep, three stories high. Back Buildings: part 13 feet 6 inches & part 16 feet wide by 81 feet 6 inches deep; two stories high; a wooden passage 3 feet by 15½ feet & Brick Privy 9 feet by 12 feet, also two stories high, the wooden passage being open below (see plan).

The Lower Story Main Building in two rooms & passage; the floor of yellow pine; moulded wash boards & surbase & wainscotted surbase high; two Clouded marble mantels with open pilasters & frieze; one breast closet & two small closets between rooms; single architraves to the windows & double A[rchitraves] to the doors, all kneed; wooden Cornice around the Ceilings & stucco Centers; two 12-light windows front, the glass 12x19, & two 15-light D[itt]o back, 14x18; all with outside panel shutters. A vestibule in the passage with folding doors, side lights, & fan sash over them & also over front door; also an arch in the passage with fluted pilasters, caps, & bases; one closet in the passage under the stairs.

The Second Story Main Building in two rooms & short passage; the floor of yellow pine; moulded wash boards & surbase & wainscotted surbase high in back room; double architraves to the doors & single A[rchitrave] to the window; kneed paneled breasts & breast closets & two small closets between rooms; two wooden mantels with carved trusses; two fluted pilasters with caps & bases at the corners of the Chimney Jambs & wooden Cornice around the Ceilings; three 12-light windows front, the glass 12x19, 7 two 15-light D[itt]o back, the glass 14x18; outside panel shutters front & back & inside shutters also back.

The third story in 3 Rooms & short passage; the floor of yellow pine; plain wash boards & surbase; single architraves to the doors & plain moulding to the windows; paneled breasts & 3 breast-closets & 3 other closets; three 9-light windows front & two back, the glass 12x16 in; outside panel shutters front & outside venitian shutters back; small wooden Cornice around the Ceiling.

The Garret in two rooms & short passage; the floor of yellow pine; plain wash boards & single architraves; two closets & 4 Dormer windows with Circular-head sash, 12 square lights, 9x12, & 6 Gothic lights in each; a Trap Door in the Roof & step ladder up to it. Stairs in the passage finished with Ramp'd mahogany moulded Rail & half Rail; turned mahogany Balusters & scroll; wainscotted handrail high with mahogany the first story & the second story is painted. These stairs lead from the lower story to the 3d story & stairs to the Cellar under them; one 12-light window on the stairs at the 2d landing, the glass 12x19; outside panel shutters; a close straight & winding stair leads from the 3d story to the Garret.

Back Building Lower story is divided into Passage, Dining Room, & two Kitchens; the floor of yellow pine; moulded wash boards & surbase; & one room & passage wainscotted surbase high; architraves around the doors & plain mouldings to the windows; panel Chimney breast, wooden mantel & mantel shelf; large dresser with doors & drawers; 5 closets; Cooking Range & Boiler; stone sink & hot & cold water; & in one of the fire places a marble slab & register. Eight 18-light windows, the glass 8x10; outside panel shutters.

The second story Back Building in 4 Rooms & two passages; the floor of yellow pine; moulded wash boards and surbase; paneled chimney breasts; one room wainscotted surbase high, architraves to the doors & plain mouldings to the windows; two large closets in the passage, & a range of closets with doors above & below in one of the Rooms; one of the Rooms is a Bath Room in which is a Bath Tub lined with copper; hot & cold water & Shower Bath; & 15 lights of Glass, 8x10 in the partitions; nine 18-light windows, the glass 8x10; outside panel shutters, a Trap Door in the Roof and step ladder.

A plain winding stair leads from the Kitchen to the second story & stairs to the Cellar under them. There is a wooden passage back which connects the Privy with the Back Building. All the windows in the main Building are double hung & all others single hung & the gas pipes plastered in, & the 1st, 2d, & 3d stories papered, except the kitchens & two small rooms over. In the Cellar are two Furnaces for warming the Building & the whole Cellar paved with Brick. Wooden

Modillion Cornice front & back of Main Building & plain wooden Cornice to back Building. Cedar Roof. Copper Gutters, lead and tin Conductors.

May 14th 1859. D. R. Knight

Surveyor

It is agreed and understood that part of the Building is to be used as a Dwelling. Liberty of Offices.

Appendix III

Description of "Governor Penn's dwelling house," which stood next to that of Samuel Powel, as provided by the survey (1428–31) made by Gunning Bedford for the Philadelphia Contributionship, August 7, 1770. The Byrd-Penn-Chew house may profitably be compared not only with the Powel House (Appendix I) but also with such contemporary Philadelphia houses as those built or remodeled for Mary Lawrence Masters, John Dickinson, William Coleman, John Cadwalader, and Alexander Stedman, surveys for which are published by Nicholas B. Wainwright in *Colonial Grandeur in Philadelphia.*

MAIN HOUSE

General description: front 30 ft.; depth 52 ft.; 3 stories; [2 rooms and a passage on each story;] painted inside and out

Facade: modillions at eaves; Ionic frontispiece

First Story

Passage: [wainscot to the ceiling;*] cornice with dentils and modillions; 2 fluted pilasters; 3 pediments [over doors]

Stairs: 2 stories of open newel stairs, ramped, bracketed, and wainscoted

Front Parlor: [wainscot to ceiling;*] cornice of fret design; 3 pediments; mantel cornice, [tabernacle] frame, etc. on [chimney] breast

Back Parlor: [wainscot to ceiling;* cornice ornamented with] Doric entablature; tabernacle frame, etc. on [chimney] breast; 3 pediments [over doors]

Second Story

Passage: [wainscot to ceiling;**] plain, double cornice; 2 pediments
[over doors]

Front Chamber: [wainscot to ceiling;**] fluted pilasters; mantel, cornice,
etc. on [chimney] breast; cornice of fret design, 2 pediments
[over doors]

Back Chamber: [wainscot to ceiling;**] cornice with modillions and dentils;
2 fluted pilasters; tabernacle frame; mantel, cornice, etc. on
[chimney] breast; 3 pediments [over doors]

Third Story   [Several rooms: each with] chimney breast, surbase, skirting,
and double cornice

THREE BACK BUILDINGS

[First]:   20 ft. by 13 ft.; 1 story; 9 in. walls, plain finish

[Second]:   40 ft. by 18½ ft. (?); 3 stories; 9 in. walls; plain finish

[Third]:   20 ft. by 18½ ft. (?); 2 stories; 9 in. walls; plain finish

The whole about ten years old.

Bedford approved insurance of £1,500 on the house and £500 on the back buildings.

* Survey says "first story wainscuted all through."
** Survey says "second story wainscuted all through."

Appendix IV

PRINCIPAL FURNISHINGS AT 244 SOUTH THIRD STREET

THAT HAVE A POWEL HISTORY

First Floor

Front Room	Three paintings on velvet in carved wooden frames	Gift of Mrs. Edward Brayton
	Pair of neoclassic bronze vases on marble stands	Gift of Mrs. Edward Brayton
	Mahogany fire screen	
Back Room	Pair of mahogany knife boxes (Fig. 63)	Gift of Mrs. Edward Brayton
	Large octagonal mahogany cellarette	Gift of Mrs. Edward Brayton
	Pieces from set of Nanking china believed to have been given to the Samuel Powels by General and Mrs. Washington	Lent by the Mount Vernon Ladies' Association of the Union
	Set of French china said to have been ordered by Samuel Powel as a gift for his wife	Lent by Mrs. Robert J. Hare Powel
	Set of French china	Lent by Mrs. E. Paul du Pont; gift of Mr. John Andrews

Second Floor

Front Room	Crimson brocade draperies	Gift of members of the Powel family
Back Room	Miscellaneous books with Powel bookplate	Bequest of Annie Brayton Powel
Other	Sewing table, said to have been given Elizabeth Willing Powel by Martha Washington	
	Child's cart	
	Sundial (Marked "SP" on back)	Lent by Mrs. E. Paul du Pont
	Sampler made in 1742	
	Scale and weights said to have been purchased in London for Samuel Powel by Benjamin Franklin	Given in memory of Harford Willing Hare Powel
	Wooden chest marked "S Powel"	

Appendix V

PRINCIPAL CONTRIBUTORS TO THE RESTORATION OF
THE POWEL HOUSE

First Floor

Passage	Restored in memory of John Cadwalader (1874–1934)
Front Door	Society of the Descendants of the Signers of the Declaration of Independence (1937)
Front Room	Mrs. John C. Martin in memory of her mother, Mrs. Cyrus H. K. Curtis (1937)
Back Room	Bridge and Tea Committee Needlework Exhibition Committee and Various Friends
Mantel and Chimney Breast	National Society of the Magna Carta Dames in memory of Ethel Nelson Page Large (1937)
Northwest Window	Modern Club of Philadelphia (1938)
Southwest Window	Jean Kane Foulke [Mrs. E. Paul] du Pont (1940)

Second Floor

Stair and Passage	Edward Ellsworth Hipsher (1937)
Front Room	Mrs. Eldridge Reeves Johnson in memory of her father, Captain George W. Fenimore (1938)

Back Room	Bridge and Tea Committee (1938) Needlework Exhibition Committee (1938)
Windows	Lydia Fisher Warner in memory of Thomas Fisher and Miers Fisher (1938)

Third Floor

Stair and Passage	Mrs. William W. Fitler in memory of William Francis Audenried (1937)
Chambers	Bridge and Tea Committee

Appendix VII

A NOTE ON THE ENDPAPERS

The endpapers reproduce a portion of the *Plan of the City of Philadelphia* originally drawn in 1796 by the surveyor John Hills and engraved in England by John Cooke.

Hills's map differed principally from the one published earlier by Matthew Clarkson and Mary Biddle in showing a variety of topographic features. Among these is the rise of ground near the Delaware River, between Spruce and Pine streets, that formed a part of the extensive holdings of the Free Society of Traders, the first stock company to operate in William Penn's new colony. Here is the origin of the name "Society Hill," used to refer to this area in the eighteenth century and again in modern times when it has figured prominently in the effort to preserve and rehabilitate the old section of the city. To the northwest, the irregular shaded areas that are accompanied by one or more black dots mark brickyards and kilns, features that become more numerous in the undeveloped western portions of the city that lie outside the section of the map used as endpapers.

As first established in 1682, the western boundary of Philadelphia extended to the Schuylkill River, but by 1800 there were still only a few scattered houses beyond Broad Street. The portion of the Hills map included here thus effectively represents the eighteenth-century city. North of Callowhill Street lay the Northern Liberties (so called because here were some of the free lots originally given to the first purchasers of land in Pennsylvania), and to the south lay Passyunk, Moyamensing, and Southwark, parts of which were shown by Hills. From an early period these outlying districts and townships were largely dependent on Philadelphia in the arts as in economics, but they were not in fact made a part of the city proper until 1854.

If much has changed since Hills published his map in 1797, much also remains the same. High Street soon came to be called "Market" in recognition of the function early assigned its eastern end. But the north-south streets are still numbered from the Delaware River, as they were from the first, and the names of trees given to the east-west streets are used today much as they were in the eighteenth century. Only Cedar Street is now called "South"; Mulberry is known as Arch; and Sassafras has become Race. George Street has also been renamed Sansom. If the endpapers show two Eighth streets, it is because until the middle of the nineteenth century the numbers ran from both the Delaware and the Schuylkill rivers to the center of town. Thus [Schuylkill] Eighth, immediately to the west of Broad Street on the Hills map, is the present Fifteenth Street.

As a convenience to purchasers of his map, Hills assigned numbers to the list of forty-eight important sites and buildings that is reproduced below with only minor editorial changes. The names of surviving structures still representative of eighteenth-century architecture are printed in italic and are further identified by being outlined in red on the accompanying map:

1. *Christ Church (Episcopal)*
2. *St. Peter's Church (Episcopal)*
3. *St. Paul's Church (Episcopal)*
4. St. Thomas' Church ("African" Episcopal)
5. St. Michael's Church (Lutheran)
6. Zion Church (German Lutheran)
7. German Reformed Church
8. Roman Catholic Chapel
9. St. Mary's Church (Roman Catholic)
10. Holy Trinity Church (German Catholic)
11. First Presbyterian Church
12. Second Presbyterian Church
13. Third Presbyterian Church
14. Friends' Meeting House
15. Pine Street Friends' Meeting and School
16. Keys Alley Friends' Meeting
17. Fourth Street Friends' Meeting
18. *Free Friends' Meeting House*
19. Seceders' Meeting House
20. Moravian Church
21. Baptist Church
22. *Methodist Episcopal Meeting House* (St. George's)
23. Seceders' Meeting House
24. Universalists' Meeting House
25. Synagogue
26. *Pennsylvania Hospital*
27. Christ Church Hospital
28. Friends' Alms House
29. University of Pennsylvania
30. German Free Lutheran School
31. Library Company
32. *Carpenters' Company*
33. *American Philosophical Society*
34. Surgeon's Hall
35. *United States Bank*
36. North American Bank
37. Pennsylvania Bank
38. *State House* (Independence Hall)
39. *City Hall*
40. *County Court House*
41. House of Employment and Alms House
42. New Theater
43. Circus
44. Gaol for Debtors
45. Gaol for Felons

46. Market
47. Fish House

48. Burying Grounds

As he confined his list to public sites and structures, Hills did not include the houses of prominent Philadelphians that figure importantly in the preceding account. To aid the reader in their identification, those that still stand have been outlined in red, and all have been assigned letters in accordance with the following list (italic designating surviving houses).

a. *Powel House* and Byrd-Penn-Chew House
b. Alexander Stedman's House
c. John Cadwalader's House
d. *Shippen-Wistar House*
e. *Reynolds-Morris House*
f. Masters-Penn-Morris House
g. John Dickinson's House
h. *Hill-Physick-Keith House*

i. Bingham Mansion
j. Benjamin Franklin's House
k. Thomas Willing's House
l. *Neave and Abercrombie Houses*
m. The Rev. Robert Blackwell's House

Though surviving, such important houses as Mount Pleasant, The Woodlands, Cliveden, Lemon Hill, and Stenton are not represented on the Hills map because they lie outside the boundaries of the eighteenth-century city.

$\mathcal{N}otes$

PART I

Abbreviations Used

HSP — The Historical Society of Pennsylvania
JSAH — Journal of the Society of Architectural Historians
PMHB — The Pennsylvania Magazine of History and Biography

1. Jefferson wrote to John Page from Paris, May 4, 1786: "The city of London, tho' handsomer than Paris, is not so handsome as Philadelphia," (*The Papers of Thomas Jefferson,* ed. Julian P. Boyd, Princeton, 1954, vol. 9, p. 445). And though he readily conceded that "in urbanity and hospitality Boston is equal to any part of America," in such matters as "buildings and furniture" Jefferson considered that Philadelphia took the lead "without doubt" (ibid., vol. 10, p. 36). The few other important Philadelphia houses that have survived *in situ* from the eighteenth century will be noted when their plans are compared with that of the Powel House; but even in their original form, the embellishments of none of these seem to have been comparable in opulence and sophistication to those provided for the Powels.

2. In the mid-nineteenth century the Powel House was numbered 258; earlier it bore the number 112. During the period under discussion, Third Street was in Dock Ward, an area bounded on the east by the Delaware River and on the south and north by Cedar (South) and Walnut streets, respectively.

3. In 1765 Charles Stedman was elected one of the first managers of the Society for the Relief of Poor and Distressed Masters of Ships, their Widows and Children, membership in which was limited to persons residing in or near the city who were or had been commanders of ships in the merchant service (*PMHB,* vol. LXXXI [1957], p. 41). See also *PMHB,* vol. LVI (1932), p. 2. Between 1737 and 1741 a Charles Stedman is listed at least three times as the master of ships sailing from Rotterdam (Ralph Beaver Strassburger, *Pennsylvania German Pioneers,* ed. William

John Hinke, 3 vols., Norristown, 1934; reprinted Baltimore, 1966). If at the age of twenty-four Charles seems somewhat young for so responsible a post, there is ample evidence that in the eighteenth century it was not unusual for even younger men to serve in this capacity.

4. Quoted by George L. Heiges, *Henry William Stiegel and His Associates,* published by the author, 1948, p. 3. On Nov. 21, 1763, Charles was the fifth among many to affix his signature to an Address of Welcome offered to John Penn as lieutenant-governor and commander-in-chief of the Province of Pennsylvania by the merchants and traders of Philadelphia (HSP, Manuscript Collection). In the eighteenth century the word "merchant" was used loosely to describe anyone engaged in business.

5. Heiges concluded that Stiegel was born in Cologne — rather than Mannheim — May 13, 1729, and that he perhaps lived somewhat longer than 1785, the year of his death given in most biographical sketches. Unless otherwise indicated, facts concerning Stiegel and his association with the Stedman brothers are taken from Heiges' account, which makes no mention of Charles's probable training as a ship's master, and speaks of both brothers as arriving in Philadelphia in 1746 after having been taken prisoner at Culloden. Edward Potts Cheyney (*History of the University of Pennsylvania, 1740–1940,* Philadelphia, 1940, p. 54) also mentions Alexander's capture.

6. Since the bar-iron produced at Charming Forge was more than Elizabeth Furnace could use for kettles, stoves, and other items of household use, much was sold elsewhere, some as far away as London (Heiges, *Stiegel,* p. 37). For additional information on the association of Alexander and Charles Stedman with Henry William Stiegel in the forging of iron in Pennsylvania, see: *PMHB,* vol. I (1877), pp. 67, 69; vol. II (1878), p. 161; vol. VIII (1884), pp. 68–69. See also *Forges and Furnaces in the Province of Pennsylvania,* prepared by the Committee on Historical Research of the Pennsylvania Society of the Colonial Dames of America, Philadelphia, 1914.

7. *Pennsylvania Archives,* 2d series, vol. IX, p. 622; Charles P. Keith, *The Provincial Councillors of Philadelphia Who Held Office Between 1733 and 1776 . . . ,* Philadelphia, 1883, pp. 157–62. Dr. Thomas Graeme (1688–1772), the son of Sir William's half-brother, had accompanied the Keiths when they came to Pennsylvania in 1717. Shortly thereafter, he married Ann Diggs, daughter of Lady Ann Keith (1675–1740) by her first husband, Robert Diggs. Sir William (d. 1749) returned to England in 1728, and in 1739 Dr. Graeme purchased his father-in-law's property known as "Horsham," situated about twenty miles to the north of Philadelphia. It was apparently Graeme who, beginning about 1755, transformed the simple stone malthouse built by Sir William in 1721–22 into a comfortable country house by the addition of suitable interior paneling and wood-

work. Today Graeme Park is administered by the Pennsylvania Historical and Museum Commission for the Commonwealth, to which it was given in 1958 by Mr. and Mrs. Welsh Strawbridge. For a full account of the house and furnishings, see: Nancy J. Wosstroff, "Graeme Park, an Eighteenth-Century Country Estate in Horsham, Pennsylvania," M.A. thesis, Winterthur Program in Early American Culture, University of Delaware, 1958.

8. *University of Pennsylvania: Biographical Catalogue of the Matriculates of the College . . . , 1749–1793*, Philadelphia, 1894, p. xi. Alexander Stedman was a trustee of the college from 1755 to 1779, when his association with all such institutions was brought to an end by his Tory sympathies ("Minutes of the Trustees of the College, Academy and Charitable Schools," vol. II, p. 145). In 1755 the Academy became the College of Philadelphia and in 1791 the University of Pennsylvania.

9. Charles Stedman was a vestryman of Christ Church from 1752 to 1774 and again from 1776 to 1778 (Louis C. Washburn, *Christ Church, Philadelphia,* Philadelphia, 1925, p. 292). He was chosen warden in 1764 and 1765 (Benjamin Dorr, *An Historical Account of Christ Church, Philadelphia,* Philadelphia, 1841, p. 298). On Aug. 1, 1754, he was one of the signers of the petition addressed to Thomas and Richard Penn, proprietaries of the Province of Pennsylvania, requesting a lot on the west side of Third Street for a church and yard

(HSP, Penn Papers, vol. 7, p. 109). For other details of Charles's contributions as vestryman and warden, see: *PMHB,* vol. XLVII (1923), pp. 343, 356; vol. XLVIII (1924), pp. 42, 45, 54, 191. Alexander Stedman served as vestryman of Christ Church from 1758 to 1766 (Washburn, *Christ Church,* p. 292); he was chosen warden in 1759 and 1760–62 (Dorr, *Account of Christ Church,* p. 297).

10. *The Philadelphia Assemblies: 1748–1948,* ed. Joseph P. Sims, privately printed, 1947, p. 10.

11. *An Historical Catalogue of The St. Andrew's Society of Philadelphia: 1749–1896,* printed for the Society, 1896, p. 15.

12. The presence of Masonic insignia on one of the stove plates produced at Elizabeth Furnace has led to the suggestion that the accompanying bust be identified as that of Charles Stedman, rather than Henry William Stiegel or George III, two more likely candidates (Heiges, *Stiegel,* p. 36).

13. Keith, *Provincial Councillors,* p. 162. Keith also mentions service by Charles Stedman as justice of the peace. Alexander Stedman's offices included: justice of the peace (Feb. 28, 1761; Nov. 27, 1757) and provincial judge (1764–67). At the time of the Revolution, both Alexander Stedman and his son Charles remained loyal to the Crown ("Minutes of the Supreme Executive Council," Aug. 31, 1777, *Colonial Records,* Harrisburg, 1882, vol. XI, p. 284). After leaving Philadelphia, Alexander is said to have gone first to New York and then to the British

Isles, where he died at Swansea (Thomas Harrison Montgomery, *A History of the University of Pennsylvania from its Foundation to A.D. 1770*, Philadelphia, 1900, p. 215). Charles Stedman, Jr., as he was known, was twice taken prisoner while serving in the British Army during the Revolution. He later wrote a *History of the Origin, Progress and Termination of the American War*, 2 vols., London, 1794 (ibid., p. 215).

14. Alexander Stedman built his house next to the one erected about four years previously by Mary Lawrence Masters, a widow whose daughter was to marry Governor Richard Penn in 1772. Rebuilt by Robert Morris after a serious fire in 1780, the Masters-Penn-Morris house at 190 High Street was selected as the Philadelphia residence most appropriate for use by General Washington during his presidency and later by John Adams during his term of office. In turning over their house as the Executive Mansion, the Morrises moved next door into the house built by Alexander Stedman, which had been seized from the Tory Joseph Galloway. Stedman had sold his house on June 9, 1770, to Israel Pemberton who on the same day conveyed it to Galloway for £2,700 (Rosamond Randall Beirne, "Two Anomalous Annapolis Architects: Joseph Horatio Anderson and Robert Key," *Maryland Historical Magazine*, vol. LV [1960], pp. 193–94). Life at 190 High Street in Washington's time is discussed by Harold Donaldson Eberlein in *Historic*

Philadelphia, vol. 43, part 1, *Transactions of the American Philosophical Society*, Philadelphia, 1953, pp. 161–78. The Late Georgian mantel and the massive lock and key for the front door, all now at the Historical Society of Pennsylvania, seem to have been the only part of the Masters-Penn-Morris house to survive its demolition in 1832.

15. Patent Deed, Apr. 21, 1760; recorded May 6, 1760, Patent Book 19, p. 515, and Exemplification Record Book 3, p. 267.

16. Since it appears on the Clarkson and Biddle map of 1762, the house to the north of the Powels' had apparently been built between that date and Feb. 23, 1761, when Thomas Willing sold the land to his sister Mary and her husband William Byrd III (Deed Book I–7, p. 276). On Nov. 27, 1764, the Byrds sold their house to Adam Hoops (Deed Book I–7, p. 278), and he, in turn, on Feb. 4, 1765, sold it to William Allen, Chief Justice of Pennsylvania (Deed Book I–7, p. 281), who gave it to his daughter Ann and her husband John Penn, Dec. 23, 1766 (Deed Book I–7, p. 283). From the Penns the property passed to Benjamin Chew, May 3, 1771 (Deed Book I–9, p. 279). The original house seems to have been replaced with a somewhat smaller one before the Chews sold the property on Jan. 28, 1828 (Deed Book G.W.R. 19, p. 374).

17. Ann Graeme Stedman (b. Jan. 1, 1725/6) died Mar. 3, 1766, and on Sept. 26, 1767, Charles married in Christ Church Margaret, widow of James Abercrombie.

The Abercrombie house (built c. 1760) on South Second Street is now restored on the exterior as the [Leon J.] Perelman Antique Toy Museum. Next to the Abercrombies lived Samuel Neave, an importer, who used part of his large house as a place of business, a common practice in eighteenth-century Philadelphia. For a sketch of how the Neave and Abercrombie houses may have appeared in Stedman's day, see: George B. Tatum, *Penn's Great Town,* 2d ed., Philadelphia, 1961, Fig. 14. Charles Stedman died Sept. 28, 1784, and both he and his first wife are buried in the yard of Christ Church on Second Street north of Market.

18. Unsuccessful in his own attempts to dispose of Elizabeth Furnace and Charming Forge, Stiegel leased from the Stedman brothers their shares of the furnace and forge in the spring of 1768, and early in the following year Isaac Cox foreclosed the mortgage which he held on the Stedmans' two-thirds of Manheim (Heiges, *Stiegel,* p. 90). In 1770 John Dickinson bought at sheriff's sale Alexander Stedman's one-third share in Elizabeth Furnace (ibid., p. 99), but Charles retained his share of the furnace until 1786 (ibid., p. 132). Despite gallant efforts to avert financial ruin, Stiegel himself was declared bankrupt in 1774 and sent to debtor's prison in Philadelphia (ibid., p. 143).

19. Powel ledger, HSP; Deed Book I–5, p. 456. The price Stedman received was £450 less than that paid by William Allen in February of 1765 for the house next door, which was similar in size but more sumptuously embellished. The "lawful money of Pennsylvania" paid by Powel was less desirable, of course, than English pounds, which were worth about one-third more. At that, Charles fared better than Alexander, who was not able to sell his house on Market Street until the following year (see note 14), though he had begun advertising it for sale in November of 1766.

20. It is not clear what Stedman meant by advertising that he could be reached at his Third Street house "by the New Building." Probably he only sought to emphasize that he had now moved and was himself living in the new house he was seeking to sell.

21. *PMHB,* vol. X (1886), p. 76. For general information about the Powel family, see: Robert C. Moon, *The Morris Family of Philadelphia,* Philadelphia, privately printed, 1898, vol. II; and Robert Johnston Hare-Powel, "Hare-Powel and Kindred Families," typescript, 1907 (HSP). The first Samuel Powell died June 27, 1756.

22. The exact date of John Parsons' first appearance in Philadelphia has not been determined, but his Certificate of Removal from an unnamed Meeting, which was recorded at the Philadelphia Monthly Meeting, is dated Sept. 4, 1681 (William Wade Hinshaw, *Encyclopedia of American Quaker Genealogy,* Ann Arbor, 1938, vol. II, p. 615). Later, he returned to England and there in

Somerset County on Aug. 23, 1685, married Ann Powell of North Curry (ibid.). By Mar. 1, 1685/6 he was back in Philadelphia, for on that date he attended the Philadelphia Monthly Meeting. "Samuel Powell" seems to have been a fairly common name, both in England and America, a fact that has contributed to a variety of genealogical errors. Partly for this reason, the parents of the first Samuel Powell to come to Philadelphia have not been identified with certainty. Possibly they were the Samuel Powle and Deborah Powle (d. Apr. 6, 1679) of Gregory Stoak, who married May 6, 1670, and to whom was born a son, Samuel, on Jan. 2, 1673 (English Friends Records, Quarterly Meeting of Bristol and Somersetshire).

23. Will Book C, p. 3, #2: 1705. The will was proved Aug. 22, 1705, when Samuel Powell and Samuel Carpenter were named as trustees and assistants to Ann Parsons in its execution.

24. Harrold E. Gillingham, "The Bridge Over the Dock in Walnut Street," *PMHB,* vol. LVIII (1934), pp. 260–69.

25. AM 10155 (folio), p. 42: transcript in *PMHB,* vol. XIII (1889), p. 248. Ann Parsons and two others had presented the young couple to the Philadelphia Monthly Meeting on Nov. 29, 1700, and on January 31 they were given leave to marry.

26. Barnabas Wilcox (Willcox) was a ropemaker who came to Philadelphia as one of the first English purchasers of land in Penn's new colony. He was buried Sept. 14, 1690 (Hinshaw, *Encyclopedia,* vol. II, p. 436) and his wife Sarah was buried on Nov. 21, 1692 (ibid.).

27. For Abigail Wilcox Powell (1679–1713), see: ibid., p. 408; and *PMHB,* vol. IX (1885), p. 240. For Deborah (1706–1729/30) and her marriage to Joshua Emlen, see: John W. Jordan, *Colonial Families of Philadelphia,* New York, 1911, vol. I, p. 193; Hinshaw, *Encyclopedia,* vol. II, p. 359; and Genealogical Society of Pennsylvania, Gen. Z, p. 182. Emlen was a tanner by trade. For Sarah (1713–1751) and her marriage to Anthony Morris, Jr., see: Hinshaw, *Encyclopedia,* vol. II, pp. 398, 626; and *PMHB,* vol. VII (1883), p. 495. Samuel Powel, Jr. was born Feb. 26, 1704/05 (Hinshaw, *Encyclopedia,* vol. II, p. 408). On his marriage to Mary Morris (1713–1759), see: *PMHB,* vol. XII (1888), pp. 487–488; and *PMHB,* vol. VII (1883), p. 495.

28. John F. Watson, *Annals of Philadelphia and Pennsylvania,* Philadelphia, 1830; enlarged by Willis P. Hazard, 1877, vol. I, p. 101. Watson's black informant also recalled that the first Samuel Powell "worked at making fire-buckets."

29. To be sure, Logan was not impressed so much with the importance of the deceased as by the suddenness with which his death occurred: "Ye 18th Instant Seventh day nite last was a week, Jn° Parsons went very well to bed in appearance & in a very few minutes was struck dead wth a Rising in his Throat, next day I was at his buring, w^thin 20 hours after I saw him walk ye Streets in good

health" (Transcript, "Correspondence Between William Penn and James Logan," 1872, vol. II, p. 58, Manuscript Collection, HSP).

30. Hinshaw, *Encyclopedia,* vol. II, p. 403. Ann Parsons' will was signed June 21, 1712, and proved Aug. 26, 1712.

31. Abigail was a beneficiary under the will of her mother, which was proved Nov. 30, 1692 (Will Book A, p. 216, #85: 1692), and she was also left £40 and one-quarter share in the residue of his estate by her brother George, whose will was proved Nov. 24, 1694 (Will Book A, p. 274 #110: 1694).

32. Carl Van Doren, *Benjamin Franklin,* New York, 1938, p. 123.

33. This rare book has been reissued by the Pyne Press as *The Rules of Work of the Carpenters' Company of the City and County of Philadelphia, 1786,* annotated with an Introduction by Charles E. Peterson, Princeton, 1971; see pp. iii, iv. The reasons for preferring 1726 to the traditional date of 1724 for the founding of the Carpenters' Company are given by Louise Hall, "Loxley's Provocative Note," *JSAH,* vol. XV (1956), pp. 26–27.

34. *The Carpenters' Company of the City and County of Philadelphia,* privately printed for the Company, Philadelphia, 1887, pp. 56, 68, 87. In 1785 a Samuel Powel is listed as a house carpenter residing on Seventh Street between Race and Vine streets, and the number of persons with this name who lived in eighteenth-century Philadelphia is a source of almost endless confusion. For example, a Samuel Powel died in 1749 (Book I, p. 231, will no. 147) and another in 1762 (Book M. p. 349, will no. 199). Neither of these appear to have any direct connection with the family here under discussion.

35. Samuel Powel, Jr. died Sept. 23, 1747, and a paragraph of his will, in which he left ground to build a meeting house, was read Oct. 30, 1747, in Monthly Meeting. In his will (Book H, p. 396, #197: 1747), the second Samuel Powel refers to himself as "junior" and provides for the unborn child his wife is expecting. Moon seems to be the source for the erroneous, but often repeated statement that Samuel Powel, Jr., died in 1759. For mention of Powel's activities as a merchant, see: *PMHB,* vol. LXVI (1942), p. 396. Samuel Powel, Jr., served on the Common Council and as an alderman.

36. Abigail Powel (b. 1735) died Nov. 16, 1797 (Moon, *Morris Family,* vol. II, p. 458). She and William Griffitts, son of James Griffitts of Philadelphia, were married April 16, 1752 (Hinshaw, *Encyclopedia,* vol. II, p. 626). Sarah Powel (1747–1773) and Joseph Potts were married contrary to the discipline of Friends inasmuch as Sarah was the first cousin of Joseph's first wife (Hinshaw, *Encyclopedia,* vol. II, p. 625). According to Moon (*Morris Family,* vol. II, p. 488), Sarah Powel Potts died Jan. 7, 1773. Hinshaw (*Encyclopedia,* vol. II, p. 408) is also the source for the third Samuel Powel's date of birth given here.

37. The first Samuel Powel's will is recorded in Philadelphia, Book K, p. 422, #274: 1756.

38. Powel entered the College of

Philadelphia on May 25, 1756 (*University of Pennsylvania Matriculates . . .*). The date of 1754 given by Montgomery (*A History of the University of Pennsylvania,* p. 548) presumably means that Powel had earlier been a student at the Academy. At least fourteen students graduated from the College in 1757, but none apparently in 1758 (*University of Pennsylvania: General Alumni Catalogue,* 1917, p. 17). At the College, Powel was a student in what was known as the "Philosophy School."

39. Carl and Jessica Bridenbaugh, *Rebels and Gentlemen,* New York, 1942, pp. 193–194.

40. Whitfield J. Bell, Jr., *John Morgan: Continental Doctor,* Philadelphia, 1965; unless otherwise indicated, details of Powel's European tour are taken from this source and from an account of Powel's life prepared by Dr. Bell for publication in a projected biographical dictionary of the members of the American Philosophical Society (hereafter cited as Bell, "Biography"). In saying that while in England Powel was elected a member of the Royal Society, Moon (*Morris Family,* p. 480) probably had him confused with Morgan or possibly with Franklin. After his return to America, Morgan was named Professor of Medicine in the University of Pennsylvania Medical School, which he had helped to establish. Later, he served on the staff of the Pennsylvania Hospital and during the Revolution as director general of military hospitals.

41. Powel left London for the Neth-

erlands June 17 and returned Aug. 31, 1761. His diary covering this period is owned by the present Samuel Powel.

42. Powel later reported that the address struck him as being a "verbose Performance" (Moon, *Morris Family,* vol. II, p. 469).

43. Dated May 11, 1763, Powel's certificate as burgess and guild brother is in the Historical Society of Pennsylvania.

44. Quoted by Moon, *Morris Family,* vol. II, p. 470.

45. The Powel-Roberts correspondence for 1761–1765 is published in *PMHB,* vol. XVIII (1894), pp. 35ff.

46. Letter of July 5, 1764, quoted by Moon, *Morris Family,* vol. II, p. 470.

47. Although it is not included in any of the studies of the painter's work with which the author is familiar, a portrait by Kauffmann was mentioned by Joshua Francis Fisher (*Recollections of Joshua Francis Fisher Written in 1864,* arr. by Sophia Cadwalader, privately printed, 1926, p. 208), and this one was so identified when it was exhibited at the Philadelphia Museum of Art in 1931 (*Pennsylvania Museum Bulletin,* vol. XXVII [1931], p. 40); on other occasions, however, it has been erroneously associated with Benjamin West. The Kauffmann portrait of Powel was previously published by Carl and Jessica Bridenbaugh (*Rebels and Gentlemen,* opp. p. 222) and by Hare-Powel "Hare-Powel and Kindred Families," opp. p. 198). Other portraits of Powel include: miniature on wood, location unknown (Theodore Sizer with the assist-

ance of Caroline Rollins, *The Works of Colonel John Trumbull,* New Haven, 1967, p. 60), and the head, sometimes attributed to Kauffmann, owned by the Philadelphia Society for Promoting Agriculture, which was formerly at the Veterinary School, University of Pennsylvania (Agnes Addison, ed., *Portraits in the University of Pennsylvania,* Philadelphia, 1940, p. 3) and is now on loan to the Landmarks Society.

48. C. P. B. Jefferys, "The Provincial and Revolutionary History of St. Peter's Church, Philadelphia, 1753–1783," *PMHB,* vol. XLVII (1923) pp. 328ff. In 1779 Powel's pew in St. Peter's was number 36. On Feb. 26, 1768, the Philadelphia Monthly Meeting disowned Powel "for having joined another Society."

49. Inevitably, many of the families who early settled Philadelphia intermarried. Edward Shippen was thus the maternal great-grandfather of Elizabeth Willing Powel, while Esther Wilcox Shippen, his third wife, was the maternal great-aunt of Samuel Powel.

50. *Recollections,* p. 208. Joshua Francis Fisher was the son of Joshua Fisher and Elizabeth Powel Francis. His mother was thus the daughter of the Tench Francis who had married Anne Willing, sister of Elizabeth Willing Powel of this account.

51. Quoted by William Sawitzky, *Matthew Pratt, 1734–1805,* New York, 1942, p. 20. The portrait of Elizabeth Willing reproduced here is not included in Sawitzky's monograph, possibly because it

was formerly attributed to Cosmo Alexander (c. 1724–1772).

52. Marquis de Chastellux, *Travels in North America in the Years 1780, 1781 and 1782,* ed. Howard C. Rice, Jr., Chapel Hill, 1963, vol. I, p. 302. François-Jean de Beauvoir, Marquis de Chastellux (1734–1788), accompanied the French forces to America with the rank of major general, but he is most often remembered as a philosopher and man of letters.

53. Ibid., vol. I, pp. 144, 168.

54. Edward Shippen was at various times Speaker of the Assembly, justice of the Common Pleas Court, and president of the Provincial Council. He is remembered principally, however, as the first mayor of Philadelphia under the Charter of 1701. The house he built about 1695 on the west side of Second Street north of Spruce was demolished in 1792, and no reliable views appear to have survived. William L. Breton (c. 1773–1855), the Philadelphia artist whose water colors have proved so helpful to historians, relied on the recollections of those who remembered the house when he painted the well-known view now preserved at the Historical Society of Pennsylvania. Esther (Hester) Wilcox (sister of Abigail, wife of the first Samuel Powell) became the third wife of Edward Shippen in 1706 (her first husband had been William Freeland and her second husband had been Philip James). When Edward Shippen, Sr., died in 1712, he left the use of his large house on Second Street to his wife, Esther, during her lifetime, and

when she died Aug. 6, 1724, the bulk of her property, including the house, passed to William (b. 1708), her son by Edward Shippen (Hinshaw, *Encyclopedia,* vol. II, p. 419). William died, unmarried, Feb. 3, 1730, at the age of twenty-two (ibid., p. 419), leaving the Shippen mansion on Second Street to his cousin Samuel Powel, Jr. (Will Book E, p. 144, #174: 1730), on whose death in 1747 it passed to his son, the third Samuel Powel and owner of the house that is the subject of this monograph. A receipt for the £80 annual rent signed by Mary Powel, mother of the Samuel Powel of this account and trustee for him during his minority, is published in *PMHB,* XXXVIII (1914), p. 243. The house was insured with the Philadelphia Contributionship (Policy 451-2). For a discussion of the probable appearance of the Shippen mansion, see Richard G. Schmidt, "Early Elegance in Philadelphia — Edward Shippen's Great House 1695-1792," M.A. thesis, University of Delaware, 1974.

55. Quoted in *PMHB,* vol. XVIII (1894), pp. 37-38.

56. Sam Bass Warner, Jr., *The Private City,* Philadelphia, 1968, p. 9.

57. Ibid.

58. Robert F. Oaks, "Big Wheels in Philadelphia: Du Simitière's List of Carriage Owners," *PMHB,* vol. XCV (1971), pp. 351-62. Much of the Cadwaladers' property was in Maryland, and doubtless others had substantial holdings outside the county and therefore not included on the Philadelphia tax lists.

59. Letter from Smith to Penn, Oct. 22, 1760 (Penn Papers, HSP), as quoted by Bell, "Biography."

60. *The Burd Papers,* ed. Lewis B. Walker, n.p., 1899, p. 184, as cited by Bell, "Biography." In considering this estimate of Mrs. Powel's wealth, allowance must of course be made for the serious inflation that accompanied the Revolution.

61. Since first published in 1873 in *The American Historical Record,* Du Simitière's list has occasionally been noted by historians. For a good recent discussion, see the article by Oaks, *PMHB,* vol. XCV (1971) pp. 351-62.

62. For further details of the carriage on exhibit at Mount Vernon, see the 1950 *Annual Report* of the Mount Vernon Ladies' Association of the Union, pp. 22-24. An account of the Powel carriage is also given by Robert Johnston Hare-Powel, "Hare-Powel and Kindred Families," pp. 199-201.

63. *The Diaries of George Washington, 1748-1799,* ed. John C. Fitzpatrick, 4 vols., Boston, 1925. During 1787, while Washington was in Philadelphia to attend the Constitutional Convention, he frequently visited the Powels; see, for example, entries under the following dates: May 17, May 20, June 15, July 4, July 16, July 27, August 22, August 27, September 13. See also: *PMHB,* vol. XIX (1895), p. 183; vol. XI (1887), pp. 302, 304, 306, 307.

64. See, for example, comments in the *Diaries* for the following days: Oct. 8, 1786, Oct. 8, 1787; Oct. 10, 1787; Mar. 29, 1788.

65. Measuring 48 by 40 inches and

long considered one of the best likenesses of Washington, the Powel portrait is signed and dated "J. Wright 1784." In the absence of any documentary evidence to support the tradition of Washington's gift, Wainwright has suggested that Mrs. Powel may well have paid the artist for it (Nicholas B. Wainwright, "The Powel Portrait of Washington by Joseph Wright," *PMHB*, vol. XCVI [1972], p. 421). Mrs. Powel left the portrait to John Hare Powel and its history from that time until its gift to the Historical Society of Pennsylvania in 1972 is recounted by Wainwright (ibid., pp. 422–23).

66. Powel to Roberts, Nov. 24, 1764 (*PMHB*, vol. XVIII [1894], p. 40).

67. Chastellux, *Travels*, vol. I, p. 131.

68. Letter to George Selwyn, June 10, 1778, quoted by Moon, *Morris Family*, vol. II, p. 481. The fact that Carlisle was on a peace mission to the colonies probably also helps to explain the cordial relationship that existed between him and the Powels. The British evacuated Philadelphia June 18, 1778.

69. Powel was elected mayor Oct. 3, 1775, and again on Apr. 11, 1789, making him the last to hold that office under the old Charter of 1701 and the first under the new one of 1789 (Moon, *Morris Family*, vol. II, p. 480).

70. *Minutes of the Common Council of the City of Philadelphia . . . , 1704–1776*, Philadelphia, 1847, p. 751.

71. Moon, *Morris Family*, vol. II, p. 480.

72. *PMHB*, vol. LXVI (1942), p. 448.

73. Powel was elected a member of the Young Junto on Mar. 7, 1760, and formally introduced on June 20 of that year (Bell, "Biography").

74. Powel was elected to the American Philosophical Society Jan. 5, 1770.

75. Bell, "Biography."

76. Edgar L. Pennington, "The Work of the Bray Associates in Pennsylvania," *PMHB*, vol. LVIII (1934), p. 21.

77. Thomas G. Morton, *The History of the Pennsylvania Hospital, 1751–1895*, rev. ed., Philadelphia, 1897, p. 418. Moon (*Morris Family*, vol. II, p. 482) mentions a contribution of $288 to the Pennsylvania Hospital.

78. *Columbian Magazine*, December, 1789, p. 783. Powel may have become interested in the dispensary through his nephew Dr. Samuel Powel Griffitts, who helped to found it in 1786.

79. In May of 1792 Powel was elected a director of the Library Company of Philadelphia, an organization founded in 1731 by Benjamin Franklin and his associates as the first subscription library in America ("Minutes of the Library Company," vol. III, p. 308), but he was not re-elected the following May (ibid., p. 331). During 1792–93 Powel also served as a trustee of the Loganian Library, the holdings of which were merged with those of the Library Company by an act of the Pennsylvania Assembly, Mar. 31, 1792 (Edwin Wolf, 2nd, *The Library of James Logan of Philadelphia 1674–1751*, Philadelphia, 1974, p. li).

80. "Minutes of the Philadelphia Society for Promoting Agriculture"

(now deposited in the Rare Book Room of the University of Pennsylvania), p. 1. Powel was made "chairman" Mar. 1, 1785, and subsequently "president" after the adoption of bylaws on March 15, a position he continued to hold until his death eight years later. Washington was elected an honorary member of the society June 6, 1785 (ibid., p. 11). The yellow fever epidemic and Powel's death in 1793 seem to have combined to end the first phase of the society's activities; the minutes end Mar. 12, 1793, and do not resume until Apr. 9, 1805.

81. Washburn, *Christ Church*, p. 292. Powel served as warden of Christ Church in 1778 and 1779 (Dorr, *Account of Christ Church*, p. 298).

82. William Stevens Perry calls Powel "one of the active spirits in the organization of the American Church after the Revolutionary War" (*The History of the American Episcopal Church 1587–1883*, 2 vols., Boston, 1885, vol. I, p. 437). For mention of some of Powel's activities in this capacity, see: ibid., vol. I, pp. 649, 655; and vol. 2, pp. 47, 66. See also, Moon, *Morris Family*, vol. II, p. 480.

83. Montgomery, *A History of the University of Pennsylvania*, p. 88.

84. Powel was elected a trustee at the meeting of the Board on June 15, 1773 ("Minutes of the Trustees of the College, Academy and Charitable Schools," vol. II, p. 65) and took his seat June 18, 1773 (ibid., p. 66). He was elected treasurer Oct. 29, 1778 (ibid., p. 111) and was succeeded by George Clymer on Nov. 18, 1779 (ibid., p. 155).

85. Moon (*Morris Family*, vol. II, p. 484) mentions two boys, both named Samuel, and this is confirmed by the stone that originally marked their grave (Edward L. Clark, *A Record of the Inscriptions on the Tablets and Grave-Stones in the Burial-Grounds of Christ Church, Philadelphia*, Philadelphia, 1864, p. 128). The dates given by Moon are:
Samuel Powel – b. June 30, 1770; d. July 14, 1771
Samuel Powel – b. June 26, 1775; d. July 12, 1775

86. Charles B. Wood III, "Powelton: An Unrecorded Building by William Strickland," *PMHB*, vol. XCI (1967), pp. 145–63.

87. Powel's will is recorded at Philadelphia in Book W, p. 569, #336: 1793. Aside from a few small bequests, he left all his property to his wife.

88. Rush mentioned his visit to Powel in a letter to his wife, Sept. 29, 1793 (*Letters of Benjamin Rush*, ed. L. H. Butterfield, Princeton University Press for the American Philosophical Society, 1951, vol. II, p. 686). Before a late October frost killed the mosquitoes that unrecognized had been the carriers of the dread disease, as many as 5,000 persons had died during the summer and early fall, bringing to a virtual stop the normal functions of the city (Richard Harrison Shryock, *Medicine and Society in America 1660–1860*, Ithaca, 1960, pp. 82, 95). See also J. H. Powell, *Bring Out Your Dead*, Philadelphia, 1949.

89. In the opinion of Joshua Francis Fisher (*Recollections*, p. 208), Powel's widow wrote his "monumental epitaph that would fill a

folio page." This is quoted in full by Clark, *Record of the Inscriptions*, p. 129.

90. The visible portions of the inscription on the urn behind Mrs. Powel read: "Dear Pledg / of Chaste & / Farewe." Also by Pratt is the unfinished portrait of Mrs. Powel earlier attributed to Gilbert Stuart and still owned by a member of the Powel family (Sawitzky, *Matthew Pratt*, p. 61). Later portraits of Mrs. Powel include that painted in 1817 by Thomas Sully, partly from a miniature by Edward Greene Malbone or Benjamin Trott (Edward Biddle and Mantle Fielding, *The Life and Works of Thomas Sully, 1783–1872*, Lancaster, Pa., 1921, p. 253; Charles Henry Hart, "Thomas Sully's Register of Portraits 1801–1871," *PMHB*, vol. XXXIII [1909], p. 164).

91. John Powel Hare was born at Philadelphia Apr. 22, 1786, and died at Newport, R.I., June 14, 1856, leaving three sons and two daughters, the survivors of nine children. After attending the University of Pennsylvania, he became a successful merchant and later served as Secretary to the U.S. Legation in London, where one contemporary described him as "the handsomest man ever seen." During the War of 1812 he held the post of inspector general with the rank of colonel in the regular army. Though elected to the Senate of Pennsylvania in 1827, his major interests in later life were the improvement of agriculture and the breeding of superior sheep and cattle. For further details of the life of John Hare Powel, see: Henry Simpson,

The Lives of Eminent Philadelphians, Now Deceased, Philadelphia, 1859, pp. 808–19; Hare-Powel, "Hare-Powel and Kindred Families"; Moon, *Morris Family*, vol. II, p. 484. Since John Powel Hare was only seven when Samuel Powel died and twelve when the house on Third Street was sold, he probably spent little time there, apart from occasional visits with his aunt and uncle. He later had built for himself two Philadelphia houses of note. The first of these was erected in 1832 on the southwest corner of Thirteenth and Locust streets, the present location of the Historical Society of Pennsylvania, which acquired the house in 1881. The second house, in the then fashionable Italianate style, was begun in 1850 in the northeast corner of Nineteenth and Walnut streets, facing Rittenhouse Square (Charles B. Wood III, "A Difficult Client," *JSAH*, vol. XXVI [1967], pp. 148–53).

92. But it was apparently John Hare Powel who, beginning about 1825–26, engaged William Strickland and possibly others to design for Powelton the somewhat heavy classical wings and portico that became its most notable features (Wood, *PMHB*, XCI [1967], pp. 150–52). For a reproduction of the Kennedy view and old photographs of Powelton, see: Tatum, *Penn's Great Town*, Fig. 66; and Wood, *PMHB*, XCI (1967), pp. 153, 154.

93. Fisher (*Recollections*, p. 209) gives as a principal reason for his great aunt's decision to move further from the Delaware River her fear of contracting yellow fever.

According to Fisher, after leaving Third Street, Mrs. Powel lived first on the north side of Market Street below Twelfth and later built an "excellent and most convenient mansion" on Chestnut Street near those of several of her relatives. Hare-Powel adds that the house on Chestnut Street in which Mrs. Powel died in 1830 was situated on the north side about fifty-seven feet east of Seventh ("Hare-Powel and Kindred Families," p. 193).

94. Deed Book E.F. 10, p. 150; consideration was £12,500 "lawful money of Pennsylvania." For an account of the Bingham family, see: Robert C. Alberts, *The Golden Voyage,* Boston, 1969.

95. Deed dated Nov. 26, 1799, and recorded Aug. 27, 1801, Deed Book E.F. 10, p. 152.

96. Deed recorded May 23, 1805, Deed Book E.F. 20, p. 388; consideration $25,000. After completing his legal studies in London, William Rawle (1759–1836) was appointed a U.S. attorney by Washington in 1791, a post from which he resigned shortly after the election of John Adams. As author of an important work on constitutional law, Rawle was made a doctor of laws by Dartmouth in 1828 (Simpson, *Eminent Philadelphians,* pp. 830–32).

97. Deed dated and acknowledged May 9, 1825, Deed Book G.W.R. 6, p. 617. The buyer was Robert Kid, merchant, and the consideration $5,000.

98. Recorded Apr. 7, 1829; Deed Book G.W.R. 27, p. 372.

99. Recorded May 1, 1829; Deed Book G.W.R. 30, p. 2.

100. Recorded Jan. 23, 1886; Deed Book G.G.P. 103, p. 204. L. Theodore Salaignac died Sept. 19, 1902, leaving a will empowering his executors to sell his real estate.

101 Recorded Dec. 30, 1904, Deed Book W.S.V. 397, p. 409; the consideration was $7,000.

102. Copies in the files of the Philadelphia Museum of Art.

103. Correspondence in the files of the Metropolitan Museum of Art.

104. The finish of the room, including the richly ornamented plaster ceiling, was purchased for the museum with funds provided by George D. Widener *(Pennsylvania Museum Bulletin,* vol. XXI [1926], p. 68).

105. The Klebanskys' gift seems to have been principally the woodwork from the two bedrooms on the third floor, "the fireplace-wall of each covered with simple, fielded panels of pine painted white" (ibid.). The museum's letter of acknowledgment is dated Oct. 26, 1925.

106. Mrs. Wolf (Chia Dora) Klebansky died July 30, 1929. For an early appeal to save the Powel House, see: H. Louis Duhring, "The Powell House," *The T-Square Club Journal,* vol. I (1931). Duhring later became architect for the restoration of the house.

107. On May 26, 1931, Wolf Klebansky conveyed the Powel House to Mildred E. Thiele, "single-woman" (Deed book J.M.H. 3318, p. 517), who conveyed it to the Philadelphia Society for the Preservation of Landmarks on July 27, 1931 (Deed Book J.M.H. 3373, p. 340). Because of the financial difficulties of the Klebansky firm, the house and lot to the south

(246 Third Street) had to be included with the sale of the Powel House, and of the $4,000 paid with the agreement of sale, $284 was advanced by Miss Wister. Funds for the final purchase came from Cyrus H. K. Curtis ($10,000) and from about two hundred interested citizens of Philadelphia and neighboring cities. By the end of 1932 the Landmarks Society had about two hundred members, of whom forty-six were "life members." Clifford Lewis, Jr., served as first treasurer of the new organization.

108. The architect for the restoration was George B. Roberts, who during 1931–32 had been among the architects who made the measured drawings of the Powel House that became a part of the Old Philadelphia Survey.

PART II

1. For an excellent outline of the English architectural tradition that lies behind the Georgian style in America, see: Sir John Summerson, *Architecture in Britain: 1530 to 1830*, 4th rev. ed., Baltimore, 1963.

2. The evidence for Wren's direct contribution to the buildings of Williamsburg is summarized by Marcus Whiffen, *The Public Buildings of Williamsburg*, Williamsburg, 1958. More recently, Alan Gowans has suggested that Wren should be considered the architect of Christ Church, Lancaster County, Va. (*King Carter's Church*, University of Victoria Maltwood Museum, Studies in Architectural History, no. 2, 1969).

3. The history of the State House is given by Edward M. Riley in *Historic Philadelphia*, pp. 7–42, and the evidence used for the modern restoration of the Assembly Room is the subject of an article by Lee H. Nelson in *Antiques*, July, 1966, pp. 64–68. The lawyer Andrew Hamilton is believed to have provided the general scheme for the State House, but Edmund Woolley was the master carpenter in charge of its construction.

4. For the history of Christ Church, see: Robert W. Shoemaker, "Christ Church, St. Peter's and St. Paul's," *Historic Philadelphia*, pp. 187–98. But though clearly in the Wren-Gibbs tradition, Philadelphia's Christ Church does not seem to have been based directly on any specific English model. Franklin helped organize a lottery to raise funds wherewith to erect the steeple.

5. Other early houses that have survived outside the old city include that built in 1707 by William Rittenhouse adjacent to his Wissahickon mill and the so-called Tom Moore Cottage, both in what is now Fairmount Park. In their essentially rural character, these simple houses belong with that built at Upland, Delaware County, by Caleb Pusey, who had come to Philadelphia in 1682 to

manage the first saw and grist mill established by William Penn and his partners. Through the joint efforts of private citizens and the Commonwealth of Pennsylvania, Pusey's house and garden have been restored and opened to the public. Unfortunately, the important Cannon Ball House (c. 1715?), is now little more than a ruin in the grounds of the city sewage plant, but further west is the early house built by Morton Mortonson (restored 1968–72) in what is now the Borough of Norwood as well as that of Thomas Massey (first portion c. 1696) in Broomall, Marple Township. Later additions and alterations have obscured the early character of Wyck in Germantown (c. 1690 but remodeled by William Strickland in 1824), Cedar Grove in Fairmount Park (1730s but doubled in size in the 1790s; moved from North Philadelphia in 1927), and the John Bartram house in West Philadelphia (begun 1655). Pennsbury, the manor on the Delaware River, near Bristol, that Penn had begun shortly after 1682 was a ruin even before the end of the eighteenth century; today it is known principally through the house and outbuildings that the Commonwealth of Pennsylvania constructed on the old foundations during the 1930s. Hope Lodge has been studied by Paul A. W. Wallace ("Historic Hope Lodge," *PMHB,* vol. LXXXVI [1962], pp. 115–42), and Stenton by Raymond V. Shepherd, Jr. ("James Logan's Stenton: Grand Simplicity in Quaker Philadelphia,"

M.A. thesis, Winterthur Program in Early American Culture, University of Delaware, 1968).

6. Edward B. Krumbhaar, "The Pennsylvania Hospital," *Historic Philadelphia,* pp. 237–46. Franklin composed the inscription for the cornerstone.

7. Charles E. Peterson, "Carpenters' Hall," *Historic Philadelphia,* pp. 96–128.

8. Louis C. Madeira, "Mount Pleasant," and Martin P. Snyder, "Woodford," *Antiques,* November, 1962, pp. 521–24 and 515–19.

9. Margaret B. Tinkcom, "Cliveden: the Building of a Philadelphia Country-seat, 1763–1767," *PMHB,* vol. LXXXVIII (1964), pp. 3–36.

10. Among the Middle Georgian country houses that once stood in the Philadelphia area should also be listed Whitby Hall, originally erected in 1754 for James Coultas on a site overlooking Ameasaka Creek in Kingsessing, West Philadelphia, and Chalkley Hall, built in 1776 at Frankford, North Philadelphia. In 1923 Coultas' descendants sold the finest portions of the interior of Whitby Hall to the Detroit Institute of Arts and used the proceeds from the sale to re-erect at Haverford, Pa., what remained of the house, though in a form somewhat different from the original. Chalkley Hall was demolished about 1955, and only the stone frontispiece, now owned by the Metropolitan Museum of Art, and perhaps a few other fragments survive.

11. In the period before the Revolution, the nearest Philadelphia came to having a colossal (giant) portico was the two-story or dou-

ble portico of Lansdowne, the house on the west bank of the Schuylkill River that was built for John Penn about 1773. After having served for a time as the country seat of the William Binghams, Lansdowne burned in 1854, though it had been painted or engraved earlier by William Birch and others (e.g., see Tatum, *Penn's Great Town,* Fig. 25). Like the giant portico, the double portico was favored by Palladio and in the American colonies used effectively in such southern houses as that of Miles Brewton (c. 1765) in Charlestown, S.C., or Drayton Hall, begun in 1738 a few miles outside the town.

12. James O. Wettereau, "The Oldest Bank Building in the United States," *Historic Philadelphia,* pp. 70–79.

13. *Philadelphia Architecture in the Nineteenth Century,* ed. Theo B. White, Philadelphia, 1953, p. 22.

14. Charles E. Peterson, "Library Hall: Home of the Library Company of Philadelphia 1790–1880," *Historic Philadelphia,* pp. 129–47. Today the library of the American Philosophical Society is housed in a building that stands on the site and reproduces the facade of Thornton's Library Hall.

15. A description of the Bingham mansion is given by Alberts, *The Golden Voyage,* pp. 162–64.

16. Virginia Norton Naude, "Lemon Hill," *Antiques,* November, 1962, pp. 531–33. In the same issue of *Antiques,* Robert C. Smith discusses briefly such lesser, but important houses in Fairmount Park as Sweetbrier, Rockland, and The Solitude.

17. The right of Philadelphia to be considered the "second city in the British Empire" is based on the earlier supposition that it had a population of 40,000 persons at the time of the Revolution, a view that more recent research has tended to disprove (Warner, *The Private City,* p. 11; Gary B. Nash and Billy G. Smith, "The Population of 18th-Century Philadelphia," *PMHB,* vol. XCIX [1975], pp. 362–68).

18. Nicholas B. Wainwright discusses "Philadelphia's Eighteenth-Century Fire Insurance Companies" in *Historic Philadelphia,* pp. 247–52, an article based in large part on his longer history of the Contributionship (*A Philadelphia Story: The Philadelphia Contributionship for the Insurance of Houses from Loss by Fire,* Philadelphia, 1952). Boston seems to have had a fire brigade as early as 1717.

19. Nicholas B. Wainwright, *Colonial Grandeur in Philadelphia: The House and Furniture of General John Cadwalader,* Philadelphia, 1964. John Cadwalader (1742–1786) was a member of a prominent Philadelphia family, a successful merchant, and an ardent patriot. His wife's fortune helped provide one of the most lavishly decorated houses in Georgian Philadelphia, and its demolition about 1820 was consequently a major loss. References to the Cadwalader house for which the source is not otherwise identified are from Wainwright's monograph.

20. See Part I, note 33.

21. Some have tried to identify the Philadelphia carpenter-architect

with a Robert Smith who came from Chester County, Pa. Most of the then-known facts concerning Smith were published by Charles E. Peterson as an appendix to his article on Carpenters' Hall in *Historic Philadelphia,* pp. 119–23.

22. William L .Turner, "The Charity School, the Academy, and the College, Fourth and Arch Streets," *Historic Philadelphia,* p. 180. In June of 1755 the trustees sought from Robert Smith, "House Carpenter," a "plan and estimate" for alterations to the Academy's Hall ("Minutes of the Trustees of the College, Academy and Charitable Schools," vol. I, p. 52).

23. Smith's work at Princeton is the subject of Paul F. Norton's opening chapter in *Nassau Hall,* ed. Henry L. Savage, Princeton, 1956.

24. It now seems that the inquiry from Philadelphia was made by Joseph Horatio Anderson (Charles E. Peterson, "American Notes," *JSAH,* vol. XVII [1958], p. 26).

25. Whiffen, *Public Buildings of Williamsburg,* pp. 162–66.

26. Thorsten Sellin, "Philadelphia Prisons of the Eighteenth Century," *Historic Philadelphia,* pp. 326–30. In the late eighteenth century, the idea of providing a place of solitary confinement where the prisoner might have an opportunity to "repent" his past misdeeds was a contribution of the Quaker community and one that formed an important part of what came to be known as the "Pennsylvania System."

27. Franklin's agent in this matter was Samuel Rhoads (1711–1784), who earlier is thought to have planned the Pennsylvania Hospital and who may therefore have advised Smith on some aspects of the design of Franklin's house. The house was demolished for a street in 1812 and no pictures of it are now known to exist (Robert D. Crompton, "Franklin's House Off High Street in Philadelphia," *Antiques,* October, 1972, pp. 680–83). For a conjectural view of how Franklin Court may have appeared from High (Market) Street in the late eighteenth century, see: Tatum, *Penn's Great Town,* Fig. 15. The history of the house is given by Edward M. Riley, "Franklin's Home," *Historic Philadelphia,* pp. 148–60.

28. Unless otherwise indicated, references to payments of craftsmen who worked on the Powel House are from the Powel ledger owned by the Library Company of Philadelphia and deposited in the Manuscript Collection of the Historical Society of Pennsylvania.

29. Pemberton Papers, HSP, vol. 22 (1770–1771), p. 146.

30. When the Landmarks Society acquired the house in 1931, there was a well in the cellar, but this has now been filled in.

31. *The Pennsylvania Gazette,* Oct. 27, 1768, p. 482. Powel paid Hale £6 7s. 6d. on Oct. 6, 1769 and £2 14s. on December 20.

32. Wainwright, *Colonial Grandeur in Philadelphia,* p. 20. Courtenay is said to have been born in Belfast, Ireland, in 1736 and at the age of twenty-six to have come to Philadelphia, where he worked in association with Benjamin Randolph (William Macpherson

Hornor, Jr., *Blue Book, Philadelphia Furniture,* Philadelphia, 1935, pp. 91–92).

33. *The Pennsylvania Gazette,* Sept. 3, 1767, p. 141; Feb. 16, 1769, p. 31.

34. *The Pennsylvania Gazette,* Sept. 3, 1767, p. 142; Sept. 24, 1767, p. 153; Oct. 27, 1768, p. 479; Dec. 1, 1768, p. 507; Jan. 12, 1769, p. 4. Hale and Reynolds were among the most regular advertisers in the *Gazette.* By 1784 Reynolds had moved to Third Street his shop known by the sign of "The Golden Boy." There he offered for sale, in addition to the looking-glasses for which he is best known, such items as Japanned waiters, trays, bread baskets, mugs, etc. (Alfred Coxe Prime, *The Arts & Crafts in Philadelphia, Maryland and South Carolina, 1721–1800,* 2 vols., Topsfield, 1929–1932, vol. I, p. 197).

35. Chastellux, *Travels,* vol. I, p. 136.

36. Sir John Summerson, *Georgian London: An Architectural Study,* New York, 1962.

37. In the simplest one-room houses the stair, a tight winder, rises in one corner beside the chimney. Next to this "bandbox" house in size is the house two rooms deep with an interior passage along one side and with a stair located in either an open or closed well between the two rooms or occasionally at the rear of the house. Larger Philadelphia houses may be thought of as essentially these two basic types, enlarged by the addition of a single file of rooms to the rear along one side of the lot. William J. Murtagh categorizes the various types of houses that made up Georgian Philadel-

phia in "The Philadelphia Row House," *JSAH,* vol. XVI (1957), pp. 8–13.

38. When preparing to live there, Washington referred to the Masters-Penn-Morris house at 190 High Street as a "Single house," by which he may have meant either that it was only four bays wide or that it shared no party walls with its neighbors (Eberlein, *Historic Philadelphia,* p. 164).

39. Isaac Ware, *A Complete Body of Architecture,* London, 1767, pp. 345–46. *The Oxford English Dictionary* defines "closet" as a small room, usually of a private nature; sometimes a bedchamber, a "closet of ease" (i.e., a water-closet), a study, or a dressing room. By a "light closet," Ware presumably meant one with a window. Ware's book seems to have been published as early as 1735–36, and of the several later editions, those of 1756 and 1767 are probably best represented in American libraries.

40. Wainwright, *Colonial Grandeur in Philadelphia,* p. 8. Since they kept some of their better china in the cupboards beside the fireplace, the Cadwaladers may have used the small front room in their house as a kind of family dining room; on the other hand, when planning to move into the Masters-Penn-Morris house, Washington thought the corresponding room there suitable for his steward (Eberlein, *Historic Philadelphia,* pp. 163, 164). Murtagh does not include the four-bay house among his four types of Philadelphia houses.

41. The survey of Franklin's house is

reproduced by Edward M. Riley as part of his essay in *Historic Philadelphia*, p. 151.

42. John F. Watson was among those who considered the cellar kitchen in Philadelphia to be a nineteenth-century development (*Annals of Philadelphia and Pennsylvania*, 1877, vol. I, p. 222).

43. Summerson, *Georgian London*, p. 31.

44. Wainwright, *Colonial Grandeur in Philadelphia*, p. 13.

45. Robert C. Smith, "Two Centuries of Philadelphia Architecture: 1700–1900," *Historic Philadelphia*, pp. 289–303. Another handsome example of a frontispiece without pediment to which Smith calls attention is that of the old north door of the Pennsylvania Hospital, now inside the present building.

46. Previous accounts usually refer to this as the Stamper-Blackwell house to accord with the tradition that it was built for John Stamper (d. 1782), a rich merchant who was mayor of Philadelphia in 1759. But since the association of the house with Stamper still awaits full documentation, in recent years it has become customary to call the house simply by the name of the Reverend Robert Blackwell (d. 1831), Stamper's son-in-law who was unquestionably living in the house by 1791. The Blackwell house was demolished about 1921.

47. *The Pennsylvania Gazette*, Feb. 13, 1766, as quoted by Wainwright, *Colonial Grandeur in Philadelphia*, p. 16.

48. Old photographs like those published by Philip B. Wallace (*Colonial Houses*, New York, 1931), show that the Powel House had been painted by the time it was acquired by the Landmarks Society, and presumably the bricks have had to be repointed more than once since first laid.

49. Though popularly known as "granite," the stone trim used for the Powel House and many other Philadelphia buildings is probably more accurately described as "gneiss-schist." It may have come from the Crum Creek quarries, from which it would have been floated up the Delaware to a convenient point on the Philadelphia waterfront.

50. Developed initially by the Romans, modillions were noted earlier as being bracket-like forms regularly used to ornament the cornices of Georgian buildings. Though rare, other types of decoration were occasionally employed in colonial Philadelphia; thus the 1766 survey of the Contributionship describes Alexander Stedman's house as having "a Dorick Eve [i.e., decorated with triglyphs and metopes] and richly ornamented." The conclusion that the present cornice is largely a replacement is based for the most part on old photographs, none of which are very clear.

51. Identification of the restored portions of the Powel House is aided by the drawings made during the early 1930s as part of the Old Philadelphia Survey of historic buildings and now deposited in the Free Library of Philadelphia. Originally intended to give employment to architects during the Great Depression, recording projects of this kind provided the impetus for what has continued as

the Historic American Buildings Survey under the joint sponsorship of the National Park Service, the Library of Congress, and the American Institute of Architects.

52. "Minutes of the Supreme Executive Council," vol. XVI, 16, p. 490 (reference from the files of the National Park Service).

53. Peter Kidson, Peter Murray, and Paul Thompson, *A History of English Architecture*, Baltimore, 1965, p. 230.

54. The word "newel" originally meant the center post that provided support for winding stairs and around which they turned. Later, by extension, it came to have essentially the modern meaning of a post that terminated the balustrade, either at the lowest step or at the landing. Because stairs were among the most difficult parts of the house to construct, whole builders' guides were sometimes devoted to the subject and considerable space was appropriately allotted to it in the *Articles and Rules* of the Carpenters' Company.

55. Wainwright, *Colonial Grandeur in Philadelphia,* p. 92. The use of a twist to terminate the balustrade at its lowest point was apparently most characteristic of the Middle Georgian period in the central and southern colonies. In the vicinity of Philadelphia it is found at Mount Pleasant; in Delaware at the Corbit-Sharp house (Odessa, 1772–74); in Virginia at Gunston Hall (Fairfax County, 1755–58); in Maryland at Montpelier (Prince George County, c. 1751); and in North Carolina at the Stanly house (New Bern, 1770) to name only a few of the examples that come most easily to mind. Though the twist was certainly not unknown further north, New England builders in Rhode Island, Connecticut, and Massachusetts are best known for the elaborately turned (or carved) newels for which there appear to be no Philadelphia counterparts.

56. Penelope Hartshorne Batcheler in an undated memorandum to the author.

57. In a letter of July 30, 1937, which was addressed to Marshall Davidson and is now in the files of the Metropolitan Museum, A. Raymond Holland, an associate of Louis Duhring and one of the architects in charge of restoring the Powel House, wrote: "We are going on the assumption that the connecting passageway on the second floor corresponds in general with the arrangement on the first floor, the original of which we have."

58. Edward I. H. Howell, grandson of Isaiah Hacker, recalled that in his day the large front chamber (which he called the "ballroom" and where he claimed to have been born) was fitted with both ivory door knobs and silver-plated hinges. In writing to Raymond Holland, Marshall Davidson, then an assistant curator at the Metropolitan Museum, also mentioned 'ivory door knobs in the room to the left of the hall on the first floor," and in May of 1929 the Philadelphia architect Erling Pedersen, in a letter to Joseph Downs at the Metropolitan, reported that he then had in his possession "an ivory knob" from one of the doors on the first

floor of the Powel House. Earlier, in replying to a letter in which J. deW. Cookman of Philadelphia (whose wife was related to the Samuel Powels) had referred to ivory door knobs, Charles O. Cornelius, Assistant Curator of the American Wing, noted that the Metropolitan Museum had found only "traces" of brass escutcheons in the room it removed. This was in December of 1924.

59. Sometime about 1914, Mrs. Lydia Bond Powel, who had just married — or was about to marry — into the Powel family, accompanied Miss Sophia Cadwalader on a visit to the Powel House, which was then owned by Wolf Klebansky. As a memento of the occasion, each woman was given a brass escutcheon from one of the doors of the house. Mrs. Powel later gave hers to the Metropolitan Museum for the upstairs room it had acquired from the Powel House and Miss Cadwalader returned hers when the Landmarks Society later undertook the complete restoration of the house. Miss Cadwalader's present is presumably the old escutcheon illustrated as Figure 37 and now on the blind door in the downstairs front room.

60. In this way the handsome Rococo marble enframement that Isaac Royall had imported for his "Best Room" was discarded in favor of white Dutch tiles when the Royall House was "restored" about 1910 (Abbott Lowell Cummings, "The Royall House in Medford, Massachusetts," *Antiques,* October, 1965, p. 506). Writing to the Philadelphia Mu-

seum in the 1930s, Edward I. H. Howell claimed to have in his house at 5218 Germantown Avenue a "black and white marble mantelpiece" which he said came from the "third story back room" of the Powel House. Efforts to trace this have thus far proved unsuccessful.

61. R. W. Symonds, "Dining Parlours and Their Furnishings," *Connoisseur,* June, 1944, pp. 92–98.

62. *Diary and Autobiography of John Adams,* ed. L. H. Butterfield, 2 vols., Cambridge, Mass., 1961, p. 127.

63. The survey of Alexander Stedman's house, which was made for the Contributionship in 1766, describes "a pantry and [a] Common Sitting Room" in one of his back buildings. By "pantry" the eighteenth century meant a room in which was kept not only bread (the original meaning of the word) but also foodstuffs of all kinds and possibly even utensils used in the preparation and serving of food. Both rooms were finished surprisingly well by modern standards: both had wainscot to the chair-rail, and the sitting room was furnished with a paneled chimney breast and a double cornice.

64. The survey of 1769 mentions only "3 Rooms on a floor," which might imply that the dimensions of "78 by 16 ft." do not include the passage, which in any case is appreciably narrower than the back building beyond. But then, surveys rarely mention passages, either because there were none or because they were taken for granted.

65. Report of Barbara Liggett, copies of which are on file at the Philadelphia Historical Commission and at the headquarters of the Landmarks Society.

66. Eberlein, *Historic Philadelphia,* pp. 163, 166.

67. "Minutes of the Committee on Museum of the Philadelphia Museum of Art for May 28, 1943," read: "It was resolved to present to the Philadelphia Society of Landmarks [sic] the woodwork from the rear ell of the Powel House as soon as the Society is in a position to install it." It is possible that there is a confusion here between woodwork of the ell and that from the three rooms on the third floor, which had been given to the museum by the Klebanskys and which was subsequently returned to the Landmarks Society.

68. The deed conveying the house on Third Street from Charles Stedman to Samuel Powel mentions, besides the house, "other valuable buildings on different parts of the . . . lot."

69. See, for example, George Strickland's view of Washington Hall, first published in *The Portfolio,* February, 1817, and reproduced in *Philadelphia Architecture in the Nineteenth Century,* Plate 16, and Tatum, *Penn's Great Town,* Fig. 53.

70. This was on Jan. 6, 1779 (*PMHB,* vol. XV [1891], p. 41).

71. Joshua Francis Fisher, *Recollections,* p. 206.

72. Wainwright, *Colonial Grandeur in Philadelphia,* p. 72.

73. The dado at Winterthur seems to be of new wood, but old photographs of the Blackwell Parlor, made before the house was demolished, show clearly the original dado with its mahogany top. Henry Francis du Pont acquired part of the woodwork from the Blackwell house now at Winterthur from the Philadelphia Museum of Art and part from the widow of J. Franklin McFadden, who had installed it in his house in Rosemont, near Philadelphia.

74. Wainwright, *Colonial Grandeur in Philadelphia,* pp. 100, 150.

75. John A. H. Sweeney, *Grandeur on the Appoquinimink,* New York, 1959, pp. 50–53. As a Quaker tanner in a rural community, William Corbit had requirements for a dwelling very different from those of the Powels. His large front chamber was called by his children simply "the long room," and at his death in 1818 it was being used as a bedroom (ibid. p. 43).

76. Wainwright, *Colonial Grandeur in Philadelphia,* p. 152.

77. Ibid. p. 150.

78. *Pennsylvania Museum Bulletin,* vol. XXI (1926), p. 68.

79. *The Pennsylvania Journal,* Dec. 29, 1763. In this advertisement Smith is called a "builder."

80. Ware, *A Complete Body of Architecture,* p. 522.

81. *Pennsylvania Museum Bulletin,* vol. XXI (1926), p. 68. As late as May 20, 1922, Alfred C. Prime in a letter to Charles Cornelius at the Metropolitan Museum reported that the ceiling remained in good condition despite the fact that Klebansky had filled the front chamber of the Powel House with workbenches used in the preparation of imported hair. Correspondence in the files of the Phil-

adelphia Museum indicates that as the workmen cut the ornament from the ceiling they glued it to canvas, using as a guide photographs made for the purpose before the operation began. Kimball probably found this method the more acceptable because of his belief that the ornament had been imported from England in the first place. J. W. & C. H. Reeves of 923–25–27 North Darien Street, Philadelphia, had the contract for this work.

82. Chippendale included subjects from Aesop's *Fables* among the illustrations in his *Director*. Though the dog on the Powels' mantel appears to be a mirror image of the same figure in the illustrations of Fable LXXX in the first edition of Francis Barlow's *Aesop's Fables With His Life* (London, 1666), the motif probably made its way to Philadelphia through one or more intermediary sources. The mantel from the Powels' front chamber is made of pine, as was customary.

83. David Stockwell, "Aesop's Fables on Philadelphia Furniture," *Antiques,* December, 1951, pp. 524–27.

84. *Pennsylvania Museum Bulletin,* vol. XXIII (1928), p. 29. Moon, (*Morris Family,* vol. II, p. 486) says that it was Theodore Salaignac (who had bought the house in 1886 and who apparently used the front chamber as his law office), who had the walls papered, and adds concerning the mantel: "It represents a hunting scene, over which is a coat of arms." Perhaps taking this or similar comments as his authority, Kimball used the Powel bookplate as the

basis for his design of the cartouche in the broken pediment of the overmantel. With the mantel the museum also obtained most of the original marble facing of the fireplace. Similar marble wherewith to restore the missing portions was given the museum by Louis Duhring (Accession No. '27–76).

85. Since he recognized that the Corbit-Sharp House at Odessa, Del., shared a number of features with the Powel House (note 75), Kimball used moldings in the former as a basis for the profiles of those he was obliged to restore when installing the room now at the Philadelphia Museum.

86. The frieze and the carved trusses were not made a part of the doors as restored in the Philadelphia Museum, though Kimball later agreed that they were appropriate additions.

87. In 1946 Daniel H. Farr, a New York dealer with offices at 11 East 57th Street, wrote Henry Francis du Pont that he recalled the original chair-rail as having been "a plain molded feature about 4″ or so wide."

88. Wolf Klebansky's bill takes the form of a letter, dated Dec. 2, 1925, in which he lists the following portions of the front room sold to the Philadelphia Museum: two mahogany doors, two pilasters, the carved mantel ("with marble facings"), the ornamented plaster ceiling, and "any other remaining woodwork" in the room. The remaining woodwork probably included door casings that are clearly visible (though without pediments) in old photographs, but not much

else. In 1926 Fiske Kimball wrote Louis Duhring that they "must surely attempt . . . at the Chapter [Philadelphia Chapter of the American Institute of Architects] to find who got the ornamental mouldings, window casings, etc."

89. From letters now at Winterthur, it appears that Daniel Farr purchased the cornice from Wolf Klebansky about 1922–23. Part he sold to James Carstairs for use in his dining room and part he installed in his own house in Chestnut Hill. A small piece (c. 18″) was obtained by Louis Duhring. In 1943 Henry Francis du Pont bought enough of the cornice from Farr for the small room now at Winterthur, and in 1926 Duhring gave his piece of the cornice to the Philadelphia Museum (Accession No. '26–54–1) as an aid in restoring the front chamber there. From Farr, or some other source, Mr. du Pont also obtained a section of the baseboard from the front chamber.

90. Letter of Sept. 27, 1927, to Fiske Kimball from White Allom & Co., now in the files of the Philadelphia Museum of Art.

91. Daniel Farr in a letter to Henry Francis du Pont, Feb. 10, 1943.

92. On Nov. 3, 1927, White Allom & Co. wrote Erling Pedersen, Kimball's assistant at the Philadelphia Museum: "With regard to the color for the Powel Room. In stripping the woodwork we found evidence of cream color underneath the applied mouldings on the mantelpiece, which evidently was the original color."

93. Wainwright, *Colonial Grandeur in Philadelphia*, pp. 23, 30. Of course some of the craftsmen employed by Powel advertised that they did gilding, and possibly the bills he paid included work of this kind that is not specified.

94. Others of Angelica's sitters hold plans, and it would be possible to compile a long list of eighteenth-century portraits that make use of this format. In some cases the drawing in question has some connection with the subject, but in other instances it apparently does not. From their respective dates it is obvious that the plan that Powel holds could have nothing to do with either his house on Third Street or Powelton, his country seat on the west bank of the Schuylkill, as has sometimes been supposed.

95. These similarities between details of the Powel House and illustrations in Swan were observed by Kimball in the course of his study of the front chamber in preparation for its restoration in the Philadelphia Museum and were subsequently published by him in the *Pennsylvania Museum Bulletin*, vol. XXI (1926) pp. 183–93. It is perhaps significant that, aside from the large pilasters that flank the chimney breasts in both large front chambers, the features that the Corbit-Sharp House shares with the Powel House are precisely the details found in Swan.

96. For example, the south facade of Mount Airy (1758–1762) in Richmond County, Va., follows closely Plate LVIII in Gibb's *Book of Architecture*, and the handsome mantel and overmantel in the "Banquet Room" of the Jere-

miah Lee House (1768) in Marblehead, Mass., is taken directly from Plate 51 of Swan's *British Architect*. Among the English books that have been convincingly identified as possible sources for details of certain Philadelphia buildings are those of James Gibbs (the facades of Cliveden and Mount Pleasant), Batty Langley (the pediment-with-mask at Belmont and Independence Hall; the Palladian window at Woodford), and Abraham Swan (mantelpieces at Mount Pleasant and Whitby Hall). But in most cases the resemblance is only a general one.

97. Alfred C. Prime, in a letter to the Metropolitan Museum, Nov. 26, 1917. In the same letter Prime also called attention to the fact that "a little of the decoration of the middle panel under the mantelpiece [had] broken off," but concluded that inasmuch as the "outline" of the missing piece was clearly visible in the old paint, it might be easily restored. In point of fact, the back room upstairs may not have been as intact as Prime supposed, since logic and the insurance surveys suggest there was probably a pediment above the door leading to the stair hall. This has been restored in the re-created room in the Powel House but not in the original, now in the Metropolitan Museum. As installed in New York, the upstairs back room of the Powel House has an ornamental plaster ceiling adapted in 1922–23 from impressions taken from the considerably larger one originally in the front room and now in the Philadelphia Museum.

98. The color favored by the Powels for the woodwork of their upstairs back room has not been determined, but in a 1949 letter to the Metropolitan Museum Miss Wister noted that its room showed "on examination to have been painted and the color is a beautiful blue." Since by the time Miss Wister wrote, all woodwork had been removed from the back room, she could only have been speaking of the plastered walls. As now installed in the museum, the original woodwork is painted a light gray and the new walls are covered with a Chinese paper.

99. The type of "single" cornice mentioned in both the survey of 1769 and that of 1785 is illustrated in Plate XXIII of the *Articles and Rules* of the Carpenters' Company, where it is appropriately priced less than a cornice of the "double" variety or than one having modillions.

100. For example, on Oct. 9, 1773, Powel paid Jacob Perkins and Abraham Heulings £70 for a "Negro woman and child," and on the same date gave William Jenkins £100 "for a Negro woman Hagar."

101. Inasmuch as Powel left almost his entire estate to his wife, no inventory may have been required.

102. Chastellux, *Travels*, vol. I, p. 136.

103. *Pennsylvania Museum Bulletin,* vol. XXVII (1931), p. 43.

104. On Aug. 10, 1771, Powel paid Thomas Proctor £3 10s. 10d. "for repairing a bookcase and stuff."

105. In 1797 Mrs. Powel bought the desk used by General Washing-

ton that is now in the Historical Society of Pennsylvania (*PMHB*, vol. XV [1891], p. 376).

106. Among the English pieces exhibited in 1931 were a mahogany table with drop leaves and a top for drafting that Franklin is said to have brought Powel from London as a gift; a mahogany shaving mirror; a hot water urn and coffee pot in the Rococo taste, which was made by Emick Romer of London (1770–71); and six candlesticks bearing the Powel crest and made in London by John Carter in 1770 (*Pennsylvania Museum Bulletin*, vol. XXVII [1931], pp. 41–46).

107. Quoted by Hornor, *Blue Book, Philadelphia Furniture*, p. 81.

108. Quoted by Harold Donaldson Eberlein and Cortlandt Van Dyke Hubbard, *Portrait of a Colonial City: Philadelphia, 1670–1838*, Philadelphia, 1939, p. 368. Powel's ledger lists a payment of £77 5s. "for Freight of sundries from London" on Nov. 10, 1767.

109. Joseph Downs, *American Furniture: Queen Anne and Chippendale Periods in the Henry Francis du Pont Winterthur Museum*, New York, 1952, Plate 30.

110. Hornor, *Blue Book, Philadelphia Furniture*, Plate 83. The museum acquired the chair in 1955; at that time it had on the back the plate which reads: "Chair from the Powel House, lent by Mrs. Edgar W. Baird." A long inventory is included among the estate papers of Samuel Powel, Jr., the merchant, but this is now in so fragile a condition that it cannot be consulted.

111. Charles Hummel, Curator of the Winterthur Museum, kindly provided this estimate.

112. *The Pennsylvania Journal*, Aug. 20, 1767. Webster advertised that prior to coming to America he "had had the honour of working with applause for several of the nobility and gentry in England and Scotland" (quoted by Hornor, *Blue Book, Philadelphia Furniture*, p. 80).

113. Prime, *Arts & Crafts*, vol. I, p. 112; vol. II, p. 146. On Oct. 2, 1769, the Powels paid John Priest £5 15s. "for a Tureen."

114. On Powel's patronage of the Richardsons, see *PMHB*, vol. LIV (1930), p. 45; and Martha Gandy Fales, *Joseph Richardson and Family, Philadelphia Silversmiths*, Middletown, 1974, Figs. 143 and 174.

115. Deed dated Sept. 22, 1769 (Deed Book D-5, p. 342); acknowledged Sept 23, 1769; recorded Jan. 4, 1783. In point of fact, the transaction seems to have been more in the nature of a trade than a sale; the cost to Powel was only five shillings, lawful money of Pennsylvania, but at the same time he rented Smith a lot on the opposite side of Third Street (Deed Book I-7, p. 312). The lot Powel thus acquired from Smith was 198 feet deep.

116. The garden of the 1930s was designed by Charles Willing; the present one is the work of Linnette M. Ott of Longwood Gardens.

117. Quoted by Moon, *Morris Family*, vol. II, p. 481.

118. The central panel of Blackwell's mantel is based on Aesop's fable

of the Dog in the Manger, but the two side ones are apparently from the stories of La Fontaine.

119. For an excellent history of the earlier phases of the preservation movement in the United States, see: Charles B. Hosmer, Jr., *Presence of the Past*, New York, 1965.

Selected Bibliography

Unpublished Sources

Bell, Whitfield J., Jr. "Biography of Samuel Powel." Unpaged manuscript for a projected biographical dictionary of members of the American Philosophical Society.

Hare-Powel, Robert Johnston. "Hare-Powel and Kindred Families." Typescript, 1907 (copy at the Historical Society of Pennsylvania).

Powel Ledger. The Library Company of Philadelphia. Deposited in the Manuscript Collection of the Historical Society of Pennsylvania.

Published Sources

Adams, John. *Diary and Autobiography*. Edited by L. H. Butterfield. 2 vols. Cambridge, Mass., 1961.

Alberts, Robert C. *The Golden Voyage: The Life and Times of William Bingham, 1752–1804*. Boston, 1969.

Bell, Whitfield J., Jr. *John Morgan: Continental Doctor*. Philadelphia, 1965.

Bridenbaugh, Carl and Jessica. *Rebels and Gentlemen: Philadelphia in the Age of Franklin*. New York, 1942.

Carpenters' Company. *The Rules of Work of the Carpenters' Company of the City and County of Philadelphia, 1786*. Annotated with an Introduction by Charles E. Peterson. Princeton, 1971.

Chastellux, Marquis de. *Travels in North America in the Years 1780, 1781 and 1782*. Edited by Howard C. Rice, Jr. 2 vols. Chapel Hill, 1963.

Cheyney, Edward Potts. *History of the University of Pennsylvania, 1740–1940*. Philadelphia, 1940.

Clark, Edward L. *A Record of the Inscriptions on the Tablets and Grave-Stones in the Burial-Grounds of Christ Church, Philadelphia.* Philadelphia, 1864.

Dorr, Benjamin. *An Historical Account of Christ Church, Philadelphia.* Philadelphia, 1841.

Eberlein, Harold Donaldson, and Hubbard, Cortlandt Van Dyke. *Portrait of a Colonial City: Philadelphia, 1670–1838.* Philadelphia, 1939.

Fisher, Joshua Francis. *Recollections, Written in 1864.* Arranged by Sophia Cadwalader. Privately printed, 1929.

Heiges, George L. *Henry William Stiegel and His Associates.* Published by the author, 1948.

Hinshaw, William Wade. *Encyclopedia of American Quaker Genealogy.* Vol. II. Ann Arbor, 1938.

Historic Philadelphia. New Series, vol. 43, Transactions of the American Philosophical Society. Philadelphia, 1953.

Hornor, William Macpherson, Jr. *Blue Book, Philadelphia Furniture.* Philadelphia, 1935.

Jefferys, C. P. B. "The Provincial and Revolutionary History of St. Peter's Church, Philadelphia, 1753–1783." *The Pennsylvania Magazine of History and Biography.* Vol. XLVII, 1923, and Vol. XLVIII, 1924.

Jordan, John W. *Colonial Families in Philadelphia.* New York, 1911.

Keith, Charles P. *The Provincial Councillors of Philadelphia Who Held Office Between 1733 and 1776. . . .* Philadelphia, 1883.

Kimball, Fiske. "The Sources of the 'Philadelphia Chippendale.'" *Pennsylvania Museum Bulletin.* June, 1926.

Madeira, Louis C. "Mount Pleasant." *Antiques.* November, 1962.

Montgomery, Thomas Harrison. *A History of the University of Pennsylvania from its Foundation to A.D. 1770.* Philadelphia, 1900.

Moon. Robert C. *The Morris Family of Philadelphia.* 3 vols. Philadelphia, 1898.

Murtagh, William J. "The Philadelphia Row House." *Journal of the Society of Architectural Historians.* December, 1957.

Naude, Virginia Norton. "Lemon Hill." *Antiques.* November, 1962.

Oaks, Robert F. "Big Wheels in Philadelphia: Du Simitière's List of Carriage Owners." *The Pennsylvania Magazine of History and Biography,* vol. XCV. July, 1971.

Prime, Alfred Coxe. *The Arts & Crafts in Philadelphia, Maryland and South Carolina, 1721–1800.* 2 vols. Topsfield, 1929–1932.

Rush, Benjamin. *Letters.* Edited by Lyman H. Butterfield. 2 vols. Published for the American Philosophical Society, Princeton, 1951.

Sawitzky, William. *Matthew Pratt, 1734–1805.* New York, 1942.

Simpson, Henry. *The Lives of Eminent Philadelphians, Now Deceased.* Philadelphia, 1859.

Snyder, Martin P. "Woodford." *Antiques.* November, 1962.

Stockwell, David. "Aesop's Fables on Philadelphia Furniture." *Antiques.* December, 1951.

Summerson, John. *Architecture in Britain: 1530 to 1830.* 4th rev. ed. Baltimore, 1963.

————. *Georgian London.* New York, 1962.

Sweeney, John A. H. *Grandeur on the Appoquinimink: The House of William Corbit at Odessa, Delaware.* New York, 1959.

Tatum, George B. *Penn's Great Town.* Rev. ed., Philadelphia, 1961.

Tinkcom, Margaret B. "Cliveden: The Building of a Philadelphia Countryseat: 1763–1767." *The Pennsylvania Magazine of History and Biography.* January, 1964.

Wainwright, Nicholas B. *Colonial Grandeur in Philadelphia: The House and Furniture of General John Cadwalader.* Philadelphia, 1964.

————. *A Philadelphia Story: The Philadelphia Contributionship for the Insurance of Houses from Loss by Fire.* Philadelphia, 1952.

————. "The Powel Portrait of Washington by Joseph Wright." *The Pennsylvania Magazine of History and Biography.* October, 1972.

Wallace, Paul A. W. "Historic Hope Lodge." *The Pennsylvania Magazine of History and Biography.* April, 1962.

Wallace, Philip B., with measured drawings by M. Luther Miller. *Colonial Houses: Philadelphia. Pre-Revolutionary Period.* New York, 1931.

Warner, Sam Bass, Jr. *The Private City.* Philadelphia, 1968.

Washburn, Louis C. *Christ Church, Philadelphia.* Philadelphia, 1925.

Washington, George. *The Diaries of George Washington, 1748–1799.* Edited by John C. Fitzpatrick. 4 vols. Boston, 1925.

Watson, John F. *Annals of Philadelphia and Pennsylvania.* 1 vol., 1830; 2 vols., 1850; 3rd vol. added 1877 by Willis P. Hazard. Philadelphia.

Whiffen, Marcus. *The Public Buildings of Williamsburg.* Williamsburg, 1958.

Wood, Charles B., III. "Powelton: An Unrecorded Building by William Strickland." *The Pennsylvania Magazine of History and Biography.* April, 1967.

Index

Unless otherwise identified, all buildings and institutions are understood to be in Philadelphia. Major contributors to the restoration of the Powel House are listed as Appendix V, pp. 135–136. Donors of principal furnishings that have a Powel history are listed in Appendix IV, pp. 133–134.

Philadelphia Georgian

has been composed in Linotype Baskerville, a modern version of the celebrated types designed in the 1750's by John Baskerville, Letter-Founder and
Printer, of Birmingham [England], who acknowledged his debt, in letter-form
models, to the types of William Caslon.

The display lines in this book are appropriately set in Caslon types, first
shown in Caslon's specimen sheet of 1734.

Benjamin Franklin admired and recommended Caslon's types, and his
own printing office was equipped with them. They became perhaps the most
widely used types in the American Colonies up to the Revolution, ultimately
yielding to types of American design and manufacture.

The type for this book was set by Connecticut Printers, Inc. The printing
was done by The Meriden Gravure Company, and the binding by Tapley-
Rutter Co., Inc. The paper is Mohawk Superfine Text, manufactured by the
Mohawk Paper Mills, Inc.